Munich

\

PETER LANG
New York • Washington, D.C./Baltimore • Bern
Frankfurt am Main • Berlin • Brussels • Vienna • Oxford

Jeffrey S. Gaab

𝔐𝔲𝔫𝔦𝔠𝔥

Hofbräuhaus & History—
Beer, Culture, & Politics

PETER LANG
New York • Washington, D.C./Baltimore • Bern
Frankfurt am Main • Berlin • Brussels • Vienna • Oxford

Library of Congress Cataloging-in-Publication Data

Munich: Hofbräuhaus & history: beer, culture, & politics / Jeffrey S. Gaab.
p. cm.
Includes bibliographical references and index.
1. Munich (Germany)—History. 2. Staatliches Hofbräuhaus in
München—History. 3. Bavaria (Germany)—History. I. Title.
DD901.M77G33   943'.364—dc22   2006019389
ISBN 0-8204-8606-X

Bibliographic information published by **Die Deutsche Bibliothek**.
Die Deutsche Bibliothek lists this publication in the "Deutsche
Nationalbibliografie"; detailed bibliographic data is available
on the Internet at http://dnb.ddb.de/.

Cover design by Joni Holst

The paper in this book meets the guidelines for permanence and durability
of the Committee on Production Guidelines for Book Longevity
of the Council of Library Resources.

© 2006 Peter Lang Publishing, Inc., New York
29 Broadway, New York, NY 10006
www.peterlang.com

Printed in Germany

All' mein' Gedanken, die ich hab,' die
sind bei dir . . .

Contents

Acknowledgments

The idea for this "short history of Munich" grew out of a seminar in European economic history at the University of Munich in the summer of 1997. A fellowship for college teachers from the *National Endowment for the Humanities* allowed me to participate in the seminar, and I am most grateful to Sheldon Hackney and Joe Neville of the Endowment. I am also very grateful to Dr. John Komlos, director of the seminar, for allowing me to participate and offering encouragement and much needed advice. Thanks are also due to Dr. Rainer Braun of the Bavarian State Archives and Dr. Anton Löffelmeier of the Munich City Archives and their staff assistants for allowing me to use the vast resources in their institutions.

So many people have helped in this project, that I apologize if I failed to mention their names here. At Farmingdale State University of New York several people helped make this volume a reality. I would like to thank the Farmingdale College Foundation. I would like to thank the Farmingdale library staff, but especially Jim Macinick, Judie Bird, Katie Thomas, and Amy Glueck for all their efforts in securing many of the German sources via inter-library loan. I would like to thank April Miller and Jane Bryan of Princeton University, Ron Roaché and Ralph Cole of the Library of Congress for helping me find out-of-print and obscure monographs on the "world's most famous beer hall" held in their collections.

I am very grateful to United University Professions/Farmingdale State University Chapter for a very generous research grant in 2001 that allowed me to visit archives in Munich that propelled this project forward. I am also very grateful to the Dean's office, College of Arts and Sciences of Farmingdale State University, and the Dean, Dr. Frank Pellegrini, who provided funds that allowed me to visit archives and libraries in the United States.

Many friends and relatives have helped with this project and I would be remiss in not mentioning them. I would also like to thank my colleagues (and mentors) at Hofstra University: Professors David Cassidy and Lou Kern. Both scholars read parts of the manuscript and offered important suggestions for improvement. The Rev. Rodney and Mitzi Eberhardt, Chris and Marion Smith read and corrected early versions of the manuscript. Gertrude Edgerly, who grew up in Munich and Bavaria and has always encouraged my work, read the manuscript and made critical suggestions for improvement. My computer and graphics experts, Sal Sciortino and Dr. Eugene Mc Coy, also deserve a word of thanks for their help. All the mistakes that remain, however, are my own.

From the moment I stepped off of the plane in Munich in 1989 as a German Academic Exchange Student, Ralf Waltram and his family have adopted me as their own. Ralf, Claudia, and the family have welcomed my wife and I to Bavaria several times over the years and instructed us in all things "*Oberbayerisch*," and we remain ever grateful. My *Stammtisch* buddy of twenty years, Norbert Strasser, taught me all I know about the *Hofbräuhaus* and *Stammtisch* etiquette. He introduced me to many other fine points of Munich life and Bavarian culture that I might have missed without the proper guide.

Patrick J. Conklin often funded research trips to Munich when grants were not forthcoming, and I am proud that I was able to introduce him to the wonders of Bavarian beer drinking culture. He is a fast learner and most accomplished pupil! Lastly, and above all, I have to thank my wife, Tara, to whom this work is dedicated. She did not realize when she married me that she would be making annual trips to Munich, yet I know that this work would not have come to fruition without her.

JSG
New York

Introduction: Munich: Hofbräuhaus *and History—* *Beer, Culture, and Politics*

The book you are holding is a short history of Munich. It did not start out that way. This project originally began as a history of Munich's famous beer hall, the *Hofbräuhaus am Platzl*. The beer hall is so intricately linked with the history of Munich, that any attempt to examine the institution leads one into the city's fascinating history. The result of such a study is a rare perspective on European history. In short, a study on the history of Munich is really a study in the development of modern Germany. Therefore, this monograph is more than just a history of a provincial city on the banks of the Isar river. Rather, this book represents an examination of German and European historical developments through the prism of Munich and its well known beer hall culture. This study assumes that there is more to the Munich story, and the history of Germany, than the Nazi experience. This book will try to illuminate other facets of German history, without attempting to denigrate in any way the significance of the years 1914–1945, with which the average reader may not be familiar.

Of all German cities, Munich stands out as one of a kind. Visitors from all over the world, and from all walks of life, have testified to the unique social atmosphere permeating the city. Munich's uniqueness arises from the city's beer culture. In Munich, all social classes and professions sat together and socialized in the great beer halls, drinking while discussing the news or current events, politics or religion. This beer hall culture translated into an almost tangible democratic environment in Munich that other German cities lacked. Historians and other observers agree that the many large beer halls in the city had a lot to do with this "democratic amiability." In Munich, the "atmosphere was so egalitarian and congenial . . . that one could almost forget one was in Germany." That contrasted sharply with "Prussian Berlin" which stood for "militaristic authoritarianism and pushy assertiveness."[1]

Munich has been known for centuries as the city of "good feeling" where anyone could live, work, fit in and enjoy life. Since at least the sixteenth century, Munich has been a center of art, music, learning and culture. Today, Munich still has some of the finest art museums, concert halls, and one of the finest universities in Europe. Nevertheless, it is that "good feeling" (the Bavarians call it '*gemütlichkeit*'), that sense of being welcome and belonging, a feeling experienced most strongly in the beer hall, that has attracted people to the city for centuries. Therefore, a study of the beer hall culture of Munich can illuminate why the city remains so popular to the present day. That is another objective of this book.

The most famous beer hall in Munich is the "*Hofbräuhaus am Platzl*" which is within walking distance of city hall. The *Hofbräuhaus* is Munich's number one tourist attraction. Few visitors realize that this famous beer hall has been at the center of German history and culture for over four centuries. Most Germans have walked through its portals sometime in their life, and hundreds of thousands of tourists from all over the world have visited the "most famous beer hall in the world." Yet aside from serving one of the most popular beers in the world, the *Hofbräuhaus* is an institution going back over four hundred years. Hence a study of the *Hofbräuhaus* in Munich is really a study of German history since 1589, the year Duke William V founded the *Hofbräuhaus* as the court's official brewery. Most of Munich's famous beer halls, such as the *Löwenbräukeller* and the *Augustinerbräukeller*, are centuries old and have played an important role in the city's history. These institutions must also be mentioned in any history of Munich. However, in this study, the *Hofbräuhaus* is used as the prototype of the local beer hall.

There are many very fine books on the history of Germany in English and many of these are used in this study[2]. Yet these books give little attention to Munich or Bavarian history. Travel books and brochures are currently the only way to get anything near a complete history of Munich or Bavaria in English. Therefore, if a student or even a tourist wanted a broader discussion of the history of Munich or Bavaria, they would have to be able to read German (or, even more daunting, Bavarian!) or be forced to search through several different historical monographs to get the full story. This study is aimed at the English speaking reader who is familiar with Munich and Bavaria and wishes to know more about this fascinating aspect of German history.

To be sure, other cities can illuminate the history of Germany. Berlin, of course, has been at the center of Prussian and German historical events for almost one-thousand years. Several books have been written on this important city, which served as the capital of Germany from 1871–1945, and serves again today as the capital of a united German nation. David Clay Large has written the most recent monograph on modern Berlin in English. In fact, in the last five years, several important books examining various aspects of Berlin's history have appeared for the English speaking reader.[3]

Munich, however, is another story. Even though the city has been the scene of important events in German and European history since at least 1158, in recent years only a few books on the history of Munich have appeared in English. David Clay Large has written an illuminating and serious book on "Munich's road to the Third Reich." Large traces the decline in the city's "democratic amiability" in the years before World War One and Munich's transformation into one of the most important cities of the Nazi movement. Gavriel Rosenfeld has written about the reconstruction of the city and its monuments since 1945. Rosenfeld shows how, after 1945, city planners rebuilt the city as close to its pre-World War Two identity as possible in an attempt to eliminate many of the reminders of the Third Reich. Both books are important for understanding Munich's experience during and after the Third Reich. These authors have exposed Munich's conflicted attempts to confront and "master" its recent past.[4] Robert Eben Sackett has written impressively about Munich's popular culture from 1900–1923. He has shown that Munich stood as Germany's most important city for cabaret life, art, and popular entertainment until the Great War's end in 1918. (Berlin achieved its cultural dominance in this area only after World War One in the 1920s). The only "recent" book in English examining Munich beyond the Nazi period is George Bailey's picture book on the city in the Time-Life "Great Cities" series.[5] A monograph on Munich with a broader historical time-frame seems warranted.

The history of a city over eight-hundred years old could easily occupy several volumes. How to manage such material?[6] The author will be forgiven for choosing to focus the study by examining Munich's history through the prism of the *Hofbräuhaus.* Generally speaking, the major historical events recorded in this book are events that, in one way or another, influenced or were influenced by, the *Hofbräuhaus am Platzl.* But the *Hofbräuhaus* is not the only beer hall in the city. Therefore, this study also examines the roles other beer halls and breweries played in the city's history. Still, emphasis will be placed on the *Hofbräuhaus* since it was the "Royal Court Brewery" and is today owned by Bavarian state.

Ludwig I (1825–1848), the King who created modern Munich in the nineteenth century, once exclaimed that his goal was to build up the city so that no one could really know Germany without having seen Munich. This book argues that in order to understand Munich, one must understand the beer culture that permeates the city to this day. This culture, a shadow of what it once was, can still be observed in Munich's surviving beer halls. The *Hofbräuhaus am Platzl* is only one such beer hall but is, in many ways, still the closest to the old style beer halls known to most Bavarians of old. If Munich is the stage upon which we watch the drama of German history unfold, then the *Hofbräuhaus* is a stage-set, a scene, to which the drama frequently returns.

Even though Duke William V founded the *Hofbräuhaus* in 1589, this study begins with the founding of the city of Munich in 1158 by Duke Henry the Lion. It will then lead the reader through Munich in the middle ages, and explore the city's role in the turbulent period of the Renaissance and Reformation. As we shall see, the *Hofbräuhaus* and Munich played important roles in the events of that period, and narrowly escaped total destruction in the Thirty Years War 1618–1648. Since the *Hofbräuhaus* experienced industrialization and expansion like many other industries, this study examines the industrial revolution of the eighteenth and nineteenth centuries in Bavaria and Munich's emergence as a modern industrial city. Naturally, the wars of recent and distant memory, and how these impacted the city, are also addressed.

Bavarians take their beer very seriously. It is impossible to understand the history of Munich, as well as the city's continuing popularity, without discussing its beer culture. Even though the Celts and the Romans brewed beer near Munich in ancient times, Munich began its ascent as the beer capital of the world only in the sixteenth century. And though there were several fine breweries in Bavaria, most of these were cloister breweries or private concerns run exclusively by monks or for noblemen. The average citizen usually brewed their beer in the home. Wealthier citizens, and the aristocracy, could afford to import their beer from the north, which had a much richer brewing tradition. However they got their beer, it is clear that beer, ale, or wine was an essential part of the Bavarian diet: water was often undrinkable.

By the sixteenth century, however, importing beer from the north became problematic for many reasons. Prices could never be guaranteed, delivery never assured, and quality could not be controlled. Therefore, in 1516, Duke William IV passed the famous "Bavarian Beer Purity Law" (*Reinheitsgebot*). From this point onward, Bavarian beer could contain only hops, barley, malt and pure water in the beer brewing process. Northern brewers had no such law so that the quality of the beer coming into Bavaria could not be guaranteed. Then, in 1517, Martin Luther posted his 95 Theses against Indulgences on the door of the castle church at Wittenberg in Saxony. The Protestant Reformation split Germany into two halves: Lutheran north and Catholic south. Good Roman Catholic Bavarians would simply not drink Lutheran (i.e., north German) beer. For these reasons (and the hope of making a profit for the court), in 1589 Duke William V, "for the good of his court," established his very own "Court Brewery": a "Hof" (court) "brauhaus" (brewery).

The court secured a supply of hops and barley, found a fresh supply of clean water, and a brew master with vast experience, Heimeran Pongrantz. By the early seventeenth century the *Hofbräuhaus* produced both the standard "brown beer" and a special "wheat beer." The beer's reputation spread so quickly, that public demand compelled the Duke to allow the local population to buy some of the beer as well. Whereas some of the locals bought the beer to bring home to drink, others began to drink right at the brewery. Therefore, the *Hofbräuhaus,* founded simply as a brewery for the court, quickly became a public house. Inadvertently, the Bavarian government had made its first venture into public hospitality. To be sure, the state sponsored lots of "high brow" culture such as building opera houses and sponsoring court musicians and composers. The founding of the *Hofbräuhaus* seems to be the first time Bavaria sponsored something so "low brow" as a pub.

There are several excellent studies on public houses and taverns in early modern Germany,[7] but it must be remembered that, at least until 1828, the *Hofbräuhaus* served as an active brewery and only secondarily as a drinking hall. Like the tavern or pub however, all social classes could be found mixing and drinking in the *Hofbräuhaus.* For the locals, the beer hall became the place to learn about or discuss the latest news or celebrate social events and holidays. The tourist and traveler usually met the local Bavarian for the first time in the beer hall. Visitors as diverse as Wolfgang Amadeus Mozart and John F. Kennedy attest to the jovial atmosphere in the world's most famous beer hall. During their visit to Munich, they joined in the revelry with the local population at the *Hofbräuhaus.* The experience of Munich and the beer hall stayed with the tourist long after they returned home. Unlike the tavern or public house, the *Hofbräuhaus* served only beer: drinkers had to find lodging and food (and other spirits) elsewhere (or bring their own). By the nineteenth century, beer had triumphed as a cultural drink that accompanied all important social events. Beer became the Bavarian's national drink and for the visitor to the beer hall it became the entrance into genuine Bavarian culture.

In 1810 Crown Prince Ludwig married Princess Therese von Sachsen-Hilburghausen. His father, King Maximillian I, gave the couple a large wedding reception on a field on the west side of town. The wedding reception came complete with horse racing, amusements, and free beer. This was the first "Oktoberfest" festival, held almost every year since in late September, early October. It remains the largest beer festival in the world. Then, in 1828, forced by popular demand, King Ludwig I opened the *Hofbräuhaus* to the general public. He added large tables and benches to the brewery, and permitted the limited serving of food. By the middle of the nineteenth century, small and large beer halls similar to the *Hofbräuhaus* had arisen all over the city. Beer had become the Bavarian's second religion. Munich became the

"Mecca"of beer in the world, and the vast beer halls that dominated the city represented the temples of this new cult. By the end of the nineteenth century, the beer hall had become so important to Munich's social scene, that all of the major breweries established large beer halls or undertook costly renovations to accommodate the demand.

But Ludwig also invested heavily in art and theater. By the end of his reign in 1848, Munich possessed some of the finest art galleries, libraries, opera houses and museums in Europe. In fact the whole city reflected Ludwig's fascination with Italy, classical culture, and learning. Throughout the nineteenth century the city attracted artists, scientists, poets and intellectuals, making it the most vibrant artistic city in Germany until World War One. Above all, however, it was Munich's beer culture, its *gemütlichkeit,* that consistently impressed visitors and observers and made it such a desirable place to live and work.[8]

No city in Europe, not even Munich, could be called the "city of good feeling" during the years of war and revolution, 1914–1945. In these years all of Europe experienced a civil war, and Munich sat in the center of the strife. The war years, and the inter-war period, marked a serious economic decline for the city. At the same time, the period witnessed a steep radicalization in politics. The first serious Communist revolution to take place in Europe outside Russia occurred in Munich in 1918–1919. In 1919 revolutionaries, imported from Russia, seized power in the city, established a "Soviet Republic," and made the *Hofbräuhaus* the "Supreme Soviet." A few months later, in February 1920, Adolf Hitler founded his National Socialist German Workers' Party on the top floor of the famous beer hall. Hitler spoke from the rostrum of the *Hofbräuhaus* repeatedly in the 1920s as he slowly built up his political movement. Plunged again into world war in 1939, Munich and the *Hofbräuhaus* suffered the same fate as the nation. By April 1945 sixty percent of the city, and most of the famous beer halls, had been destroyed by bombs. By 1945, Munich's Jewish culture had been all but destroyed. It took local *Müncheners* twenty years to rebuild most of the city, though only about thirteen years to rebuild the *Hofbräuhaus,* as close as they could to its pre-1945 appearance. But many of the scars remain.[9] Today, Munich is Germany's most popular city and the *Hofbräuhaus* is its number one tourist attraction.

This study, then, uses the *Hofbräuhaus* and Munich's other beer halls as a sort of microscope to examine the course of Germany's history since the twelfth century. It is hoped that the reader will discover that there is much more to Munich and its famous beer hall than just beer. This book argues that the *Hofbräuhaus,* and the city of Munich, can teach us much about German history and culture. The *Hofbräuhaus am Platzl,* in the heart of old Munich, stands as a living monument to Germany's fascinating history.

1. *Religion, Politics, and Beer:*
The Origins of Munich's Hofbräuhaus

Bavaria, and the area that would later become Munich, was originally settled by the Celts. The name of Munich's famous river, the Isar, is originally a Celtic name meaning "the river that rises" (*"Die Reißende"*) since it regularly overflowed its banks. In 15 B.C. Roman armies arrived pushing the Celts out of the area.[1] By the seventh century Christianity had already taken root in the area, and monks and monasteries existed throughout Bavaria. The native "Bajuwaren" or Bavarians that lived in the area were dominated by foreigners, the Franks. In the eighth century Charlemagne (761–814), the Frankish king that united all of Western Europe under his control, incorporated Bavaria into his empire. He deposed the Bavarian ruling family and awarded the province to his political vassals. After Charlemagne's death, Bavaria remained on the eastern most fringes of the former empire and was later incorporated into the Holy Roman Empire that formed in central Europe under Otto of Saxony in 962. The last of the foreigners to rule Bavaria, and the founder of the city of Munich, was Duke Henry the Lion (*Heinrich der Löwe*), 1129–1195.[2]

The monks that populated the area were scholars and generally men of peace: teachers as well as priests. That, combined with the wealth usually concentrated in their cloisters, made them favorite and easy targets for invaders, especially the Hungarians, who invaded central Europe in the tenth century.[3] Legend has it that the monks of *Schäftlarn,* on the left bank of the Isar, were forced to abandon their monastery and flee the invading Huns, taking refuge down river in improvised huts. This settlement later became "Monichen" or "München" a sort of nick- name meaning "where the monks are."[4]

At the time of its founding in 1158, Munich seemed in no way destined for greatness. Freising, the ecclesiastical city to the north, was at least four hundred years older than Munich, far more richer and, as the seat of the arch-bishop, far more powerful. Augsburg, Regensburg, and Salzburg were all ancient cities dating from Roman times. Even after its founding, Munich remained a small, almost backwater settlement by comparison.[5]

Munich was founded in the days when *Friedrich Barbarossa* ("the Red Beard") was Holy Roman Emperor. Even before he was elected Emperor, however, he promised to award the duchy of Bavaria to his cousin, Henry the Lion. Henry, who had established several market towns throughout Germany including Lübeck in the north, had long had designs on Munich. His goal was to establish a city "by the monks" and use it to seize control of the salt trade from Otto, the powerful Archbishop of Freising. But the Arch-bishop was also a relative of the Emperor, so Henry could not simply ask for those rights. If he wanted control of the salt trade in south Germany, Henry would have to take it by force. This was not just a family squabble, it was a serious political conflict as well.

After clandestinely building up the "monk's settlement" as a market town, Henry invited merchants and traders from all over Germany and Europe to come and set up shop. He also established a mint at the site so that the city was ready to take over the salt trade just as soon as the Emperor approved it, which was by no means a sure thing. Finally, he built a fortified bridge across the Isar river, linking the city with Salzburg, to facilitate the transport of salt. He struck at the opportune moment. In 1154 Henry destroyed the bridge over the Isar which Archbishop Otto maintained near Freising. Anyone now wanting to ship salt from Salzburg to northern Germany would have to go through Munich, over Henry's bridge. The Arch-bishop protested angrily to the Holy Roman Emperor, but in vain. Emperor Frederick needed Henry's support for a military campaign in Italy. After the successful campaign, meeting in Imperial Diet at Augsburg on 14 June 1158, Frederick confirmed Henry's control of the salt trade in southern Germany and officially recognized his city "by the monks:" Munich. To placate the Archbishop, Emperor Frederick ordered Henry to send one-third of all his profits to the Archbishop of Freising. The birthday of the city is celebrated on this day every year.[6]

To ensure that his interests were protected in the new city, Frederick Bar-barossa appointed one of his trusted servants from the Palatinate to Henry the Lion's court, a Bavarian named Otto von Wittelsbach. During a later mil-itary campaign in Italy, Emperor Frederick called on Henry the Lion for sup-port. Henry, having gotten what he wanted, this time refused to help the Holy Roman Emperor. Outraged, Frederick summoned Henry before an Imperial Tribunal at Regensburg at which Henry refused to appear. Conse-quently (in 1180), the Emperor and princes of the Empire voted to depose him as Duke and award Bavaria, and Munich, to the Pfalzgraf Otto von Wittelsbach. The Wittelsbach family ruled Bavaria and Munich for the next 750 years, until November 1918.[7]

In the Middle Ages, Bavaria was known particularly for bad wine, not beer. Breweries were either privately operated by monasteries, or they were the purview of the local lord, who alone had the authority to grant a brewing license. In fact, the earliest breweries in Munich were associated with religious institutions. The *Augustinerbräu* was founded by Augustinian monks in Munich in 1328. The *Weihenstefan* brewery, the oldest continuous brewery in Bavaria, was also part of a monastery and was founded in the year 1040 near Freising. Generally speaking, Europe's best beers came from northern Germany, from cities such as Einbeck, Hamburg, or Bremen. In northern Germany, breweries were licensed by the city or community and therefore that beer was usually produced for commercial consumption all over Europe. The Swedish Bishop Olaf Magnus once claimed that beer in Europe always tasted better the further north one traveled.[8]

The Archbishop of Freising's wounds must have healed sufficiently because in 1188 he allowed a church to be built in Munich: St. Peter's Church, which quickly became one of the symbols of Munich and is known today simply as "Old Peter" (*Alte Peter*). Munich quickly became a major trading city, dealing in goods from as far away as Italy. In fact, some of the residents of the city at this time came from Italy and traded in such items as wine and textiles. Jewish influence in the city was already prominent by the twelfth century. The credit, loan, and money changing services they provided made Munich a very easy place to do business and a center for trade in southern Germany.[9]

Munich grew rapidly throughout the thirteenth century. In 1240 the Holy Roman Emperor restored all market rights and privileges to the city. In 1253 the first imperial residence, known today as the "Alte Hof" was finished, and the Wittelsbach family took up permanent residence in the city. In 1271 city fathers erected a "chapel" to the Virgin Mary which later became the Cathedral of Our Lady (in 1468). In 1255 however, after the death of Otto II, his sons divided Bavaria between themselves: Ludwig II made Munich his official capital while Heinrich I made his capital at Landshut. Until the early sixteenth century Bavaria then had two capitals and two rulers. In 1315 the (Munich) Duke of Bavaria, Louis "the Bavarian" (*"Ludwig der Bayer"*) was simultaneously elected Holy Roman Emperor. Munich therefore became an imperial city. The official colors of the city became black and gold as these were the official colors of the Holy Roman Empire and the Emperor. During his reign, in 1327, fire raged through the city, destroying the Alte Hof and St. Peter's Church, and left at least one-third of the city in soot and ashes. Ludwig undertook the reconstruction of the city personally, greatly expanding it, and laying out the first battlements and city walls.[10]

What fire could not do, the Black Plague did. The Bubonic Plague reached Europe from China in 1347. By June 1348 the pestilence reached Munich and Germany. Some argued that sin caused the sickness, others insisted the Jews brought on the disease. Groups of radical penitents called the "flagellants" (named after the whip used by the Romans) roamed from town to town whipping themselves as penance in hopes of alleviating the disease. They often blamed the Jews for causing the disease, and pogroms against the Jews were organized in Munich in 1349 and throughout Europe as the plague spread. Between 1348 and 1680 there were at least twenty-five major epidemics of plague in the city, wiping out significant numbers of the population. In 1633, the residents of the picturesque town of *Oberammergau* vowed they would reenact the passion and death of Jesus Christ every ten years if God spared the town from plague. The "Oberammergau Passion Play" has been preformed by residents of the town every decade since. The plague forced Munich and most cities throughout Europe to improve sanitation and health conditions as best they could. Careful attention had to be paid also to beer brewing, since drinking the water was out of the question.[11]

Even though Emperor Frederick Barbarossa seems to have passed the first law aimed at ensuring quality in beer brewing, it was only after the first attack of plague that the brewing of beer was formally regulated. In 1363, to guarantee quality and purity, the Munich City Council took over the duty of supervising and regulating the production of beer throughout the city. Part of the regulation was to ensure that beer was produced within the city (and that it could therefore be taxed) but also to ensure that it was healthy.[12] Emperor Frederick declared that "a brewer who makes bad beer or pours an unjust measure shall be punished: his beer shall be destroyed or distributed at no charge to the poor." Above all, beer had to be fresh. However, without modern methods of refrigeration, it was difficult to keep beer fresh throughout the year. Therefore, in 1553 Bavarian authorities outlawed the brewing of beer in summer. From 1553 until the late nineteenth century, brewing could only be performed "from St. Michael's Day until St. George's Day" essentially from September 29 until April 23.[13]

The first formal beer purity law passed in 1487 applied to all beer brewed in Munich. In 1493 a second purity law was passed that applied to all of Bavaria ruled from Landshut. After 1503 the two branches of the Wittelsbach family were united, and all of Bavaria was ruled from Munich. Therefore, on April 23, 1516 the two beer purity laws were combined into one that applied to all of Bavaria. The law declared that only hops, barley, and water could be used in the production of beer. All substitutes and any other preservatives were strictly forbidden. This is the first and oldest law regulating the quality of a consumable item in the world.[14]

In 1468 the most prestigious architect in Munich, Jörg von Halsbach designed and built the most visible landmark in Munich, the famous *Frauen-dom:* The Cathedral of Our Lady. By this time Munich had become a large enough city to merit its own bishop. To pay for the building, the Pope approved the sale of indulgences. Sixty-five thousand people flocked to the city of Munich to obtain the plenary indulgence and help build the magnificent new church.[15] Several years later, in the fall of 1510 an Augustinian monk, Martin Luther, stayed in the Augustinian monastery not far from the cathedral on his first (and only) pilgrimage to Rome. According to witnesses, Luther preached a "good Papist" sermon and, we can surmise, enjoyed the very fine beer brewed at the monastery.[16] (Luther was no stranger to fine beer: Luther's wife, Katherina von Bora was an excellent beer brewer, earning her license at Grimma in Saxony, where she had served as a nun before leaving the cloister to marry the reformer. Later in life, in 1535, Luther declared that beer gave him the strength to fight the devil: "I much rather drink a tankard of beer against the devil so that I can despise him!")[17]

Something happened to Luther in Rome however that changed him forever. On 31 October 1517, a few years after his return from Rome, the same Dr. Martin Luther posted his "95 Theses Against the Sale of Indulgences" on the door of the Castle-Church at Wittenberg, where he was also Professor of Scripture at the University. Originally the Church granted indulgences for free to entice crusaders to go off to the Holy Land to fight Muslims. An Indulgence granted the crusader remission of time in purgatory if killed in battle. By Luther's time however, the selling of indulgences to the laity had been authorized by Pope Leo X to finance the building of St. Peter's Basilica in Rome. Even before the indulgence sellers invaded Germany from Italy, the papacy had sent hundreds of monks and emissaries selling everything from relics, miracle cures, and pardons in order to raise funds for an increasingly insatiable papal court. In fact, by Luther's time, Germans regarded all of these traveling clerical-salesmen as "riffraff going back and forth across our land, begging, collecting, offering indulgences, and extracting large sums of money from our people." Luther's protest against the selling of indulgences spread rapidly throughout the German-speaking lands thanks largely to the printing press. Luther's students quickly translated his 95 Theses into German, had hundreds of copies printed, then sent them all over Europe. To many Germans, Luther seemed to be the voice they had longed for, a leader who could reassert Germany's freedom from Rome. Luther vocalized what many Germans despised about the medieval papacy: the increasing extortion of money from the German faithful, and the political encroachments of the Holy Roman Emperor.[18]

Luther's Reformation, which in his eyes was strictly religious, aiming at reform of the Church, quickly became a political movement which divided

Germany and Bavaria. For example, in 1525 Luther's writings inspired a large scale peasant revolt. Peasants demanded that serfdom and slavery be abolished, that they be allowed to choose their own pastors and break free of the power of the bishops. Riots and armed revolts broke out all across southern Germany that the Princes bloodily suppressed. Luther was horrified by the bloodshed, but heartily supported the Princes. He authored two essays "The Admonition to Peace" and "Against the Robbing and Murdering Hordes of Peasants."[19] The Peasant's Revolt was brutally suppressed and Lutheranism failed to take hold in southern Germany. And that was only the beginning of the violence. As the Reformation heated up, and Germany chose sides, tolerance went by the board. As Lutherans ransacked monasteries and churches in north Germany, the Roman Catholic pious sent what holy relics could be salvaged south to Bavaria. The bones of St. Benno, Bishop of Meissen, were sent to Munich at this time and St. Benno became the patron saint of the city. Hundreds of people who followed the new faith in Munich had to flee; some of these were hand workers and craftsmen, some even members of the nobility. All had to flee north to the protestant areas of Germany. Between thirty and fifty Lutherans were murdered in the city between 1523–1527 and the numbers of persecuted rose as the battle lines hardened.[20]

German beer now became part of the controversy. For the Bavarian Dukes, beer not only had to be pure in content, it had to be pure in God's eyes as well. Duke Wilhelm V imported beer for his court from Zschopau, near Chemnitz, and Einbeck (the famous "bock" beer), which came from near Hannover: Lutheran territories! Lutheran beer was in the mugs of Catholic royalty! The staunchly Roman Catholic Wilhelm, who eventually entered a cloister himself and was known as "*der Frommer*" ("The Pious,") could not tolerate this situation. Moreover, there were over six hundred members of the Bavarian Court, and importing beer from such distances became extremely expensive.[21] A popular ditty at the time went:

> In Bavaria there was a Duke
> Who had an awful thirst.
> He also had many servants
> Whose thirst was even worse.[22]

Quality control also became an issue. Brewers in the north were known for using malt and hops substitutes in their export beer. Aside from the bad taste, use of substitute ingredients violated Bavaria's strict beer purity law. If the beer from the north did not reach Munich, or it was delayed, the court went dry or it had to drink the inferior local brew. Something had to be done!

On September 27, 1589 the Bavarian nobility requested "for the good of the court" that a court brewery be established. After a cost analysis, Duke

Wilhelm V formally accepted the proposal and, four days later granted permission for construction to begin that same autumn. The nobility at court had already worked out most of the logistical problems. Hops could be obtained from Bohemia and brewing equipment could be easily purchased. The main concern was finding a brew master that could produce a quality beverage. It appears that, even before the Duke's approval, they had secured the services of a brew-master, Heimeran Pongratz, who became the first brew master of the *Hofbräuhaus*.[23]

The brewery was to be erected right on the grounds of the court. Old bath houses were removed and a beer cellar dug out. After some construction delays, the first brown beer started to appear in the court brewery in 1591. The beer was served in liter mugs or "steins" (though one asked not for a stein but a "*maß*" or "measure" of beer) the German word for clay out of which the mugs were made.[24] A few years later, in 1603 the Duke was able to reserve to himself and the court brewery the exclusive right to brew *Weissbier*, a sweeter white beer made with wheat. Thus, in 1603 a "w*eissbierbräumeister*" Hanns Ammann, worked along side the "*braunbierbräumeister*" Pongratz. In only a few years it was clear that the brewing quarters had become too crowded. Therefore, in 1606 the *weissbier* brewing operation was moved around the corner to the *Platzl*, where the Duke had been steadily buying up property since 1585. This is where the *Hofbräuhaus am Platzl* stands to this day.[25]

The oldest brown-beer invoice that has been preserved, dating from 1605, records a total of 2, 256 buckets of winter and summer beer, 705 buckets of which were sold to the general public. The Duke and the court began to make a substantial profit from their beer. As early as 1604 *Hofbräuhaus* beer began to sell outside of Munich and was exported to Straubing, Landshut, and Regensburg.[26] In 1610 the Duke permitted the *Hofbräuhaus* to expand its business and sell its beer to the general public on a regular basis. Local innkeepers were then permitted to buy beer at Court and sell it to the general population of the city. Still, the nobility at court missed their northern "Ainpockisch" (strong beer from Einbeck). In 1614 Pongratz's successor as brew master, Elias Pichler, experimented and produced a similar beer which he brewed throughout the winter and released only in Springtime, around May. This beer came to be called "Maibock" (May Bock Beer), a slightly stronger brew that really pleased the court and the locals.[27] *Hofbräuhaus* beers had become famous by this time, developing a local and regional reputation for quality. Then the Thirty Years War erupted.

Whereas in northern Germany the aristocracy used Luther and the Reformation to break from the control of the Papacy and the Holy Roman Emperor, in Bavaria the opposite occurred. The Bavarian Duke became the champion of the Papacy and Roman Catholicism, and leveraged that support to gain concessions from the Viennese Holy Roman Emperor and the Vatican.[28] Southern Bavaria became a center for Roman Catholic opposition to the Protestant Reformation in Germany. Duke Albert V (ruled 1550–1579) had churches inspected annually to make sure the Protestant heresy was nowhere to be found, and he censored all Protestant literature, ordering the works of Martin Luther burned. The Duke refused permission for Bavarians to study abroad, lest they come into contact with the heresy and bring it back to Bavaria. The Duke also invited the Order of the Jesuits into Bavaria to take over the administration of schools and universities. The Jesuits, founded by the Spanish friar Ignatius of Loyola in 1540 had, by the sixteenth century, become the vanguard of the counter reformation in Europe. When Protestant noblemen from northern Bavaria tried to protest these measures, Duke Albert expelled them from the Bavarian Diet. Thereafter, Albert and his successors became, for all intents and purposes, absolute monarchs in Bavaria. By 1609, Protestants and Catholics had formed rival political and military alliances throughout Germany. Protestant states formed the "Protestant Union" which was headed by the Elector and Duke of the Palatinate, a state just to the west of Bavaria. Roman Catholics founded the "Catholic League," headed by the Duke of Bavaria who, after the Holy Roman Emperor Ferdinand II von Habsburg, became the single most powerful Catholic prince in Germany.[29]

War between the two forces broke out in 1618 after a Protestant led rebellion in Bohemia. The war lasted on and off for thirty years. Ferdinand paid the Duke of Bavaria handsomely to raise an army in 1620 and attack the Protestant forces in Bohemia. At the Battle of the White Mountain, the Bavarians quickly defeated the Bohemians and the Duke of Palatine's forces. The title of Elector was now taken from Frederick of Palatine and granted to Maximilian I, Duke of Bavaria. From that point forward, the Bavarian Dukes held the right to vote on the election of the Holy Roman Emperor. By 1629, with the help of a rogue army led by a soldier of fortune named Albrecht von Wallenstein, the Holy Roman Emperor almost succeeded in uniting all of Germany as a Catholic empire under Habsburg control.[30] Had he been successful, the German people might have been unified in a single nation-state three hundred years before Bismarck accomplished the feat in 1871.

But the Protestant forces soon rallied. Neighboring powers in Europe watched German developments with concern. France, under the statesmanship of Cardinal Richelieu, grew anxious as the Austrian Habsburgs gained more territory and assembled a formidable empire in central Europe. Richelieu desperately sought a way to stop the Habsburg advance and reassert French influence in Germany. Sweden was by this time firmly in the Lutheran camp. The King of Sweden, Gustavus Adolfus, feared the annexation of the

Protestant areas of Europe by Roman Catholic forces. "As one wave follows another in the sea" he is said to have remarked, "the papal deluge is approaching our shores." Therefore, in one of the more ironic twists in seventeenth century politics, the Catholic Cardinal Richelieu agreed to help finance a Lutheran Swedish army to stop the Habsburg expansion in Germany. Sweden then invaded Germany in 1630 to help rescue the Protestant cause in Europe. In 1631 at Breitenfeld, Adolfus smashed the Catholic forces and by April 1632, at the Battle of Lechfeld, Adolfus reversed all of the Catholic gains up to that point, and reasserted Protestant hegemony in Northern Germany. Bavaria and Munich now lay before him, ripe for the taking.[31]

Munich had been working on its fortifications for several years, but they were still not ready when Adolfus struck. Intending to take a terrible revenge on the city in exchange for the burning of (Protestant) Magdeburg at the beginning of the wars, Swedish forces entered Munich on May 17, 1632. The Swedes exacted no such revenge, however. After their invasion of the city, no murders, no plundering, not even arson took place. The Swedish forces remained very well behaved. In fact, Gustavus Adolfus was fascinated with the city. As soon as he arrived in Munich he went sight-seeing, stopping to chat with local *Müncheners*, even entering into debate with the Jesuit priests (reportedly in fluent Latin) assembled in front of St. Michael's Church to greet him. He liked the city. "Munich," the King of the Swedes declared, was "a golden saddle on a very scrawny horse."[32] After a lengthy meeting with a delegation from the city, and after French intervention, Adolfus agreed to spare the city in exchange for 300,000 Thalers. By the time his full occupation force arrived on June 7, 1632, Munich had only raised a third of the sum. In a compromise, Gustavus Adolfus authorized the taking of several hostages until the money was paid, and accepted 220 hectoliters of the now famous *Hofbräuhaus* brown beer, and several liters of the bock beer to spare the city.[33] *Hofbräuhaus* beer saved the city of Munich from total destruction in the Thirty Years War.

The real suffering that came to Munich as a result of the Thirty Years War came about unintentionally. Spanish troops were brought in to reinforce the city after the Swedish retreat. They brought with them the bubonic plague, and the pestilence ravaged the city for a second time. One third of the population of Munich died as a result.[34] The gains made by Bavaria in the Thirty Years War came almost just as unintentionally. Even though in Europe the war resulted in a draw (with the north remaining Lutheran, the South Roman Catholic and western Germany a mix of Lutheranism, Roman Catholicism, and Calvinism), Bavaria emerged stronger and larger, if still religiously divided. At the Peace of Westphalia, which ended the Thirty Years War in 1648, Bavaria received part of the Palatinate, and the Bavarian Dukes retained the title of "elector." The violence and hatred that began before the war continued well after 1648. Between 1575 and 1591 forty people were executed for "protestant heresy." In 1590 the first witchcraft trials were held in the city, and by 1600 over four-hundred people had been arrested, hanged or burned at the stake. Whole families were reportedly burned together in the city center. Witch burning in the city finally ended only in 1721.[35]

After the Thirty Years' War, other wars continued to rack the continent, only the causes of war had changed. Whereas in the seventeenth century nations fought over religious issues and convictions, in the eighteenth century they fought over influence, territory, and power. And again, Germany, Bavaria, and Munich were caught in the middle. The years 1701–1714 marked the War of the Spanish Succession. Bavaria sided with France against the interests of Austria. Austrian armies defeated the Bavarians at the Battle of Höchstätt, and Munich was occupied by Austrian forces in 1705. On Christmas night, 1705 the people of the city, and farmers from the outlying areas, marched through the city protesting the quartering of Austrian troops. The Austrians, in response, murdered eight-hundred of the protesters outside the Sendlinger Gate on the west side of the city. The occupation finally ended in 1711 and the city celebrated by building a new church, the Church of the Holy Ghost, right next to St. Peter's Church on the *Talstraße*.[36] By this time Munich and Bavaria had become famous for their beautiful houses of worship, some in Gothic, but many now in Italian-baroque style. The historian Gordon Craig has written that what Johann Sebastian Bach was to the Lutheran Reformation, Italian baroque architecture was to the Catholic Counter Reformation in Bavaria. The Cajetan Church or St Michael's Church in Munich, and the *Wies Kirch* in Upper Bavaria, were all built in this period. These baroque masterpieces represented a new status and fame for Bavaria and a resurgent Roman Catholicism in southern Germany and Europe.[37]

This fame would also extend to its beer. The Thirty Years War had essentially destroyed the Hanseatic League and its distribution system in northern Germany. This made it extremely difficult to sell or distribute northern beer in southern Germany or throughout the continent. Moreover, climate conditions had resulted in a sever shortage of wine.[38] With the competition destroyed, and wine becoming ever more expensive, Bavarian beer and the *Hofbräuhaus* stepped in to fill the demand.

2. From Occupation to Oktoberfest: Munich becomes a World City, 1715–1828

The Austrians left more than bad feeling and casualties after their occupation of Munich in 1705: they left coffee. That caffeinated drink from Africa and Asia had slowly made its way to Europe and, only after the Austrian occupation, seems to have made an impact on the citizens of Munich. By 1726 there were at least seven coffee houses in the city.[1] The new drink was a sign of the changes taking place in Munich, Bavaria, and Europe in the eighteenth century: factory labor and mass-production. The beer brewers of Munich, many of whom sat on the city council, tried desperately to stop the importation of the drink into the city. As more people turned away from beer and embraced the new drink, they feared coffee would cut into their profits. But coffee became more and more popular as factories and mass production began to emerge in Europe. These factories were essentially large plants where hundreds of workers manufactured products and consumer goods. Caffeinated drinks began to replace beer as the drink of choice and facilitated the transition from farm to factory. Caffeine helped factory workers stay awake during long hours in the factory or get up before sunrise to make it to work on time. This became especially important by the nineteenth century as machines were added to those factories and when falling asleep at work could be dangerous if not fatal.[2] Invalids, unskilled workers, poor women and children often made up the bulk of the workforce in this period.[3] Though "machines" were still in the future, manufacturing plants and factories emerged all over Europe, marking the end of the cottage industry and guild system, and preparing the way for the industrial revolution.

According to one observer traveling through Munich in the eighteenth century, it was "the prettiest city in all of Germany." At the time, the city possessed about 1,676 houses and buildings, and if one included the royal residences and palaces, the city had close to 1,700 dwellings. Fire protection was afforded by roughly 8,829 fire stations. At night, the main streets at least were illuminated by about 600 gas lanterns. The observer noted that he had never seen such beautiful girls and women anywhere else in Europe.[4] Above all, a visitor in Munich or Bavaria at this time would have noticed the beauty of its churches. Every architectural style and art form was to be found in Munich's churches from late Romanesque and Gothic, to Baroque and Rococo. What the observer would not realize was that over half of all the land in Bavaria was owned by the Roman Catholic Church or one of its religious orders. This severely hindered the duke's ability to finance state operations since, according to ancient custom, the church and its many religious orders paid no taxes. The wealthier the Catholic Church became, and the more churches it erected, the more the cry began to be raised that the church pay its fair share.[5]

In Europe, this was the period of the "Enlightenment" or the "Age of Reason" where thinkers began to emphasize the power of reason and science over faith. It was during this period that the *Illuminati,* a semi-secret society dedicated to the pursuit of knowledge and "reason" was founded at the University of Ingolstadt. Comprised of young university professors, students, and civil servants, the *Illuminati* demanded social reform from the ground up, and a state organization based on the rule of law rather than ancient privilege. Famous members of the *Illuminati* movement included Johann Wolfgang von Goethe, Johann Gottfried Herder, and many of Germany's most famous philosophers. The *Illuminati* championed the Enlightenment ideas of Rousseau, Voltaire, and Montesquieu, and revered the accomplishments of the American and French Revolutions. It was through the *Illuminati* that Enlightenment reforms would be accomplished in Bavaria.[6]

The impetus for reform was accelerated by the new ruler. In 1777 the last Wittelsbach of the old Bavarian line, Maximilian III Josef died. Worse, he died childless. In 1778 Karl-Theodor von der Pfalz, a member of the Wittelsbach family from the Rhineland provinces, was able to secure the throne, and moved his seat from the Pfalz to Munich. As soon as he arrived in Munich he began to remake the government in his own image. He entrusted his reforms to his chief privy councilor: Benjamin Thompson, Graf von Rumford.

Benjamin Thompson (1753–1814) was an American. Born in Rumford (now Concord) New Hampshire, Thompson fled the American colonies when he failed to get a permanent commission in the colonial army. Instead, he joined the British army toward the end of the American War of Independence, and when that conflict ended in 1783 he made his way to England, France and finally Munich. Impressed with his skills as a commander, the

Elector elevated him to the rank of "Baron of the Holy Roman Empire" and gave him the title Count von Rumford. At the height of the French Revolution when class tension threatened all of Europe, Rumford established the city's first police department. Rumford was also responsible for consolidating the Bavarian and Pfälzer branches of the army, creating a modern national army for Bavaria.[7]

Rumford also began the first state welfare system in the city. He eliminated beggars from the streets of Munich by cleaning and feeding them, then putting them to work on all kinds of public works projects sponsored by the state. While in Munich he also served as Minister for War, Minister of Police, and Court Chamberlain. His greatest accomplishment, however, was to plan and over see the construction of Munich's famed "English Gardens" one of the most beautiful recreation spots in Munich and Europe to this day.[8] Originally planned as a soldiers' field, it was decided instead to create a public park since communing with nature and natural beauty were all virtues praised by the Enlightenment. In the spring of 1792 the English Gardens officially opened to the public. On 1 April a food concession was added by the Chinese Tower near the center of the garden[9] which is Europe's largest public garden. Today, there are statues to Rumford on the *Maximilianstraße* and a Rumford Square near the *Isartor* subway stop. The beer concessions in the English Gardens today are operated by the *Hofbräuhaus*.

Of course the revolution in philosophy and politics which the Enlightenment caused spread to many other areas of knowledge as well. Music, for example, underwent fundamental changes in the eighteenth century. One of the greatest musical innovators of the period, Wolfgang Amadeus Mozart, lived in Munich in a house directly opposite the original *Hofbräuhaus* in 1780–1781. Mozart was so moved by the place that he wrote a poem about the famous beer hall and the city entitled "Among All Cities":

> Of all the cities in which I stayed
> made much music and my instruments played
> I once took up residence in Munich.
> I gave a fine concert there at court,
> the opera Idomeneo in 1780 there I wrote,
> and often sought refreshment in the Duke's brew house.
> The beer there really pleased me
> and the guests never ceased to amuse me
> Anyone who's been there would agree with me![10]

Looking back on his days in Munich, Mozart would declare that "in all truth I amused myself too much . . ." This was a criticism leveled by his father, who seemed never to believe that Mozart was working hard enough. In fact, Munich was a very prolific time for Mozart. In addition to the opera, Mozart also composed several short vocal works, three piano sonatas and an oboe quartet. And this was not Mozart's first association with the city. At age six he had given a recital for the Elector, Maximilian III Josef, and in 1775 the Elector commissioned an opera from Mozart ("La Finta Giardiniera") for that year's *Mardi Gras* season. In fact, in 1777 Mozart had approached the Elector, asking for a position as court composer, but he failed to secure the position. Again in 1780, the year he actually took up residence in the city, Mozart had been invited to Munich by the Elector Karl Theodore to write an opera for the 1781 Mardi Gras season. He arrived in 1780, taking lodging on the *Burggasse* very near the Court and the brewery. Within months Mozart had completed the opera "Ideomeneo" which he considered his greatest work. Mozart hoped, as did his father, that the opera would finally result in Mozart's commission as Court Composer to Elector Karl-Theodor. By all accounts the premiere of the opera was a huge success, but the commission from the Elector never materialized.[11] Such a commission might have put Munich on the map as a premiere cultural city for music in the same rank as Vienna or London. In 1785 Mozart's *Die Entführung aus dem Serail* was the first opera ever performed in German at Munich. One historian has called the failure to offer Mozart a commission Karl-Theodor's greatest blunder. Karl-Theodor died in 1799.[12] *Die Entführung* sparked some of the first (German) nationalist feelings in the Bavarian populace. Napoleon Bonaparte would do the rest.

The same year that Napoleon Bonaparte came to power in France, Prince Maximilian IV Josef became Duke and Elector of Bavaria, in March 1799. The Duke's wife, Karoline Fredericka von Baden was a Protestant. Therefore, one of the first reforms Maximilian IV. Josef effected was to eliminate the law requiring membership in the Roman Catholic Church for state service. He also allowed the construction of Protestant churches in Bavaria. Queen Karoline donated the first Protestant Church to be built in Munich: the St. Matthew's Church on the *Sendlingerstraße,* and this served as the "mother church" and is the seat of the Protestant bishop of Bavaria.[13]

Even though Munich had been a center (one might even say the headquarters) of the Roman Catholic Counter Reformation, and the spearhead of Catholic forces in the Thirty Years War, Bavaria had been home to many Protestants who could prove their worth to the ruling family. Count von Rumford, for example, was a Protestant. Once, when Rumford fell ill, hundreds of townspeople gathered outside his house to pray for him. Many of these were the poor and indigent he had strived to help, and he was overwhelmed by their concern. "Imagine," he wrote, "public prayers for me! For a private person! A stranger! A protestant!" In any case it was not the "Catholics" that drove Rumford from Munich but rather jealous noblemen. In 1798 he left Bavaria as Ambassador to England.[14] Another famous Protestant (and also American) family in Bavaria at this time, and working for the

Elector was Baron Jacobus von Washington, a distant cousin of the first President of the United States of America. The Washington family had fled England during the period of the English Civil War and the Cromwell dictatorship 1646–1660. John Washington (George Washington's grandfather) fled to Virginia with his brother Lawrence and a cousin, James Washington. James later left the colonies and made his way back to Europe, settling first in the Netherlands, then Germany. Elector Maximillian elevated Jacobus to the position of hereditary knight in his personal service as military advisor. By the time he died in 1848 he had risen to the position of commander-in-chief of the Bavarian army and Grand Chamberlain. Duke Maximilian became the Godfather to Jacobus' son, Maximilian von Washington, who later took up service to the monarch of Austria-Hungary.[15]

Maximilian IV Josef's chief political advisor was Prince Maximilian Montgelas. He was determined to reform the political and social structure of Bavaria, basing many of those reforms on the reforms effected by the French Revolution. Above all, Montgelas wanted to strengthen the power of the state administration over and above the privileges of the Bavarian aristocracy and the church: to make Bavaria a modern state. His aim was to reform the law code to ensure equality of all before the law, reorganize and modernize the court system and bureaucracy, decrease the power of the princes and provide for freedom of religion by secularizing much of the property of the Roman Catholic Church.[16]

Montgelas was also a member of the *Illuminati,* that group of reformers that had been waiting to have their chance at modernizing the Bavarian state. Montgelas required all Bavarian children to attend school, eliminated the tax privileges and social benefits of the nobility, moderated punishment in the penal system, and outlawed witch burning.[17] Montgelas abolished serfdom and slavery. By this time Napoleon had increased his influence in Germany by reorganizing all of the states along the French border and ensuring that they were loyal to France. Opposition to Montgelas' reforms, especially from the aristocracy or clerical classes, Napoleon and his army helped to suppress. Moreover, Montgelas was a French émigré (with Bavarian roots on his mother's side) so France was eager to help one of its own remake Bavaria in the French revolutionary image. That is not to say that it was because of Napoleon that Maximilian IV Josef and Montgelas carried out their reforms. Rather, Napoleon's control of Germany unleashed reform forces that had been brewing for a long time. Geopolitically, Napoleon radically transformed Germany. In 1803 Napoleon issued his famous *"Reichsdeputation-shauptschluß"* by which he reorganized, eliminated or otherwise consolidated the states of the German speaking areas of Europe, excluding Prussia and Austria. Out of 138 kingdoms and principalities, duchies, and ecclesiastical states, Napoleon created 35.[18]

With Napoleon as protector, the Montgelas' domestic reforms went on full force. Bishoprics, abbeys, cloisters, and convents were now confiscated by the state, the contents sold, sent to museums or libraries, and sometimes the lands were sold. The church was brought almost totally under the control of the state and its influence in politics substantially reduced. In 1808, Maximilian issued the first constitution for Bavaria, based heavily on the French model.[19]

As French power increased on Bavaria's western border, it became clear to the Bavarian elector that he would have to accommodate French expansion if Bavaria were to survive. Max Josef had served in the French army and had an affinity for France and the Corsican Emperor. Therefore Duke Maximilian IV Josef formally allied with the French in 1805. Napoleon defeated the Austrian Habsburg empire that same year, and the mighty Prussian empire a year later, in 1806. This brought to an end what the Germans called the "first *Reich*": the "Holy Roman Empire of the German Nation" which had existed since 962. Napoleon then completely redrew the borders of Germany and reorganized central Europe to his pleasure. Napoleon visited Munich twice in 1805 in October and December and the city was forced to house several thousand French troops. Some families were even compelled to house 50 or 60 men at a time which spurred lots of anti-French sentiment, but no outright rebellions.[20] Bavaria was, for all intents and purposes, occupied by the French.

Nevertheless Bavaria profited handsomely from French victories. Bavaria received many of the ecclesiastical cities of the former Holy Roman Empire, especially Augsburg, Regensburg, Passau, and Freising to name but a few. Having "captured" Freising, the Archbishop was "moved" from Freising to Munich: Munich's "Cathedral of Our Lady" (*Frauendom*) became the seat of the Archbishop and the Roman Catholic Archdiocese of "München-Freising." Thanks to Napoleon, by 1806 the Wittelsbach family controlled the entire geographic area from the Alps in the south, to Frankfurt am Main in the North, bordered by Austria in the east, and Württemberg and Baden in the west. And, because of Max Josef's loyalty, Napoleon elevated Bavaria to a Kingdom: on January 1, 1806. Duke Max Josef became King Maximilian I of Bavaria.[21] Napoleon solidified his alliance with Bavaria by marrying his stepson, Eugene Beauharnais to the Bavarian princess Auguste Amalie in the same year.

From 1806 on, until the end of World War One, the *Hofbräuhaus* was known as the *Königliches Hofbräuhaus:* the Royal Court Brewery. Under the Montgelas' reforms, guilds were abolished and freedom of profession introduced. Now, if one wanted to be a brewer, all that was needed was a license from the state, not approval by a guild. The reforms called for the abolition of church and cloister breweries so that secular places like the *Hofbräuhaus* became even more important to the city. For a cloister to maintain its brewery, two conditions had to be met. First, the brewery must itself be on the grounds of the cloister. Second, the cloister must be active and have inhabitants. Moreover, brewers now had to pay a "beer tax" after 1806 and in 1811 a "Uniform Beer Price" law was passed so that private brewers could not sell beer on the cheap and decrease the yield of the beer tax.[22]

Demand for *Hofbräuhaus* brown beer rose so quickly in this period, that the small brewing quarters at the court were simply not large enough for the operation. Therefore, in 1808 the brown beer brewing operation was moved around the corner to the *Platzl,* joining the white beer brewery at that location. *The Hofbräuhaus* brewery was now entirely located on the *Platzl.*[23] The first mention of the area known as the "*Platzl*" appears on maps only in 1780. Up until that time the area was known as the "Graggenau" quarter. In addition to the *Hofbräuhaus* brewery operation, a "Bockbierkeller" was also established on the Platzl. Thus, by the nineteenth century the *Platzl* became the headquarters for beer drinking in Munich.[24]

Beer was becoming big business in Munich and it was about to get bigger. In 1805 regulations on who could brew beer had to be established. With the "*Minutoverschluß*" decree, the King declared that inn keepers and tavern owners could only buy beer from breweries (not make there own). Breweries could sell their beer cheaper than the inns and taverns, but they could not serve food (customers could bring their own food if they so chose). This kept both the breweries and tavern keepers happy.[25] Thus, in the eighteenth century beer halls, which were still really only breweries, began to take on the function of the tavern or public house. Larger than the local tavern, the beer hall also emerged as the centers of democracy in Bavaria. In the beer hall the soldier and priest, butcher and baker, civil servant and farmer all sat together: there was no class, or sex segregation of any kind. Women were there in large numbers, some in fancy dress, others "bare headed" and common. Democracy and beer, beer and the good life came to be synonymous with the *Hofbräuhaus* and Munich in this period. It was where the spirit of freedom and democracy could always be found. *Gemütlichkeit,* that uniquely Bavarian mixture of fun and hospitality, was born.[26]

And if there was not ample room within the beer hall, there was room just outside. In the eighteenth century, as the population of Munich grew ever larger, so did the demand for beer. The problem was how to brew enough beer and anticipate demand, which was almost impossible. The solution was to brew excess beer and hold it in reserve, but how to store it and keep it fresh? The solution was the beer garden or beer cellar. Without refrigeration, the beer had to be stored in a cool, dry environment. Breweries then built cellars to store reserve quantities of beer. To keep the cellars cool, they planted chestnut trees over the cellars which, with their large green leaves, kept the ground (i.e., the tops of the cellars) in the shade and cool. Now, in the eighteenth century brewery owners began to place their empty barrels in the garden and, if patrons so chose, they could drink their beer, standing in the garden in the shade of the chestnut trees, especially on warmer days.[27]

To celebrate the wedding of his son, Crown Prince Ludwig, to Princess Theresa von Sachsen-Hilburghausen, King Maximilian declared a week of games and horse racing on the "wiesen" or meadow on the west side of town just outside the Sendlinger gate. The marriage took place on 12 October 1810, the games began on 17 October 1810. The first "Oktoberfest" was born. The Munich Chamber of Commerce had been in discussion with the King about holding a "Maximilian Week" which would include a children's carnival with rides and games. In addition to the games and the carnival, the King allowed free beer for the entire week. This was the first Oktoberfest in Munich, and has been held the last week of September and first weekend in October almost every year since.[28]

Beer and wine graced the festival almost from the beginning. In 1815 the first beer concessions were permitted. Added to the beer concessions were rides, music, food, and games. In 1818 the first carousel was installed. Beer consumption and the number of visitors increased yearly so that, by 1835, over 100,000 people visited the Oktoberfest and 250,000 liters of beer were consumed. In 1865 one observer noted that "The Fest began punctually at 2:00pm. The biggest Ox I have ever seen. The meadow and environs filled thick with people. Beer from a thousand barrels. Bavaria celebrates, endless carousing. All Munich is one big beer barrel."[29]

The Oktoberfest quickly came to be seen as a national festival, where Bavaria showed off its cosmopolitan, live-and-let-live culture, its "*gemütlichkeit.*" It is also around this time that the wearing of a national costume or *Volkstracht* became widespread. The costume consisted generally of leather pants or shorts and suspenders, elaborately embroidered shirts and pressed wool or "loden" coats, hats or outer wear. By 1800 three distinct types of this "lederhosen" can be identified: For men "Cullotes" which are leather pants that tie just below the knee (*Bundhosen* in German), long leather shorts that usually came to the top of the knee (*Lederhosen*), and shorter shorts that ended just above the knee. Women began to wear elaborate dresses with colored aprons and hats called *Dirndls*. Local variations of the costume, such as the color or the pattern of stitching, designated a particular locality, region or group. In 1883 the first national association for the organization and preservation of "*Volkstracht*" was founded. In 1835, for the twenty-fifth wedding anniversary of King Ludwig I and his wife Theresa (and therefore to commemorate the first Oktoberfest) the first *Volkstrachten* parade was organized. Since 1950, this parade occurs every opening weekend of Oktoberfest.[30] (The Oktoberfest has been cancelled only 25 times in its

180 plus years of observance. Twenty-three times because of wars, and twice, in 1854 and again in 1873 due to cholera outbreaks. One terrorist attack by Neo-Nazis occurred in 1980). By the 1890s, the Oktoberfest was directed more and more by the big Munich breweries and less and less by the Chamber of Commerce.[31]

Bavaria suffered 30,000 casualties participating in Napoleon's campaign in Russia in 1812. By 1813 it was clear that Napoleon would not go down in history as the emperor who had freed Europe from centuries of aristocratic repression, but rather as the first modern dictator in European history. Having received assurances from Prussia and Austria that Bavaria would not be annexed for originally supporting France, and that he would not loose any of his royal privileges, Maximilian officially switched sides in 1813.[32] At the Battle of Leipzig, Austrian, German (with Bavarian troops) and Russian armies decisively smashed the French forces, forcing Napoleon's retreat to France and, ultimately, his surrender in 1815.

Perhaps rethinking his commitment to reform in light of the Napoleonic episode, in 1818 King Maximilian issued his second, more conservative constitution. The constitution established a bicameral legislature and also included a statement of basic rights and freedoms for the Bavarian people. Still, only the lower house of parliament was elected, and voting was still severely limited by economic class and social status. The king appointed the cabinet and approved the members of the upper house.[33] Even though most political power remained in the hands of the King as supreme commander of the army and head of state, the ground had been laid for Bavaria's emergence as a modern industrial state. As if to solidify Munich's leading role in the modernization of Bavaria, in 1826 King Maximilian I ordered that the University of Landshut be formally relocated, with all its faculty and students, to Munich. (The king duly compensated the city of Landshut, once one of two Bavarian capitals). Munich was now the undisputed intellectual capital of the nation.[34]

In 1818 Maximilian commissioned one of the most beautiful buildings in all Munich: the Royal Court or National Theater. It was and remains one of the most beautiful theaters and opera houses in Europe. However, less than four years after its grand opening, in January 1823, the magnificent structure caught fire. Because the water normally used to fight fire was frozen solid, firemen rushed to the *Hofbräuhaus* in an attempt to gather barrels of beer in hopes of quenching the fire. To no avail: the building burned to the ground.[35]

"Old Max," Bavaria's first king, finally died in 1825. Bavaria lamented the death of its first monarch who had raised Munich to a truly cosmopolitan capital and cultural center and more than just a great place to drink beer. In the nineteenth century, under his successor Ludwig I, Munich would become a major art center and a technological hub of an emerging German nation. Beer and the *Hofbräuhaus* would be at the center of all of these momentous changes.

3. *The Reign of the Ludwigs: 1828–1897*

Ludwig I built the modern city of Munich. He ascended the throne in 1825 and ruled until 1848. In this period he rebuilt the city in his image, and that image was Italian. Ludwig was particularly fascinated by Florence. During his lifetime Ludwig visited Italy some fifty-two times. The buildings erected during his reign, from the new university buildings on the *Ludwigstraße*, to the impressive museums he built to store as much Italian and Renaissance art as he could acquire, were constructed in Italian-Renaissance style.[1] Standing on the *Odeonsplatz*, one has the feeling of being in Florence.

Ludwig wanted to share with the public all that he had seen and collected on his many trips to Italy. Therefore, in 1826 Ludwig laid the foundation stone for the *Alte Pinokothek* to display his vast collection of ancient Greek and Roman art. Today it remains one of the world's richest art museums. Ludwig's interest in Greece stretched also into politics. He supported the Greeks in their struggle for independence from the Ottoman Empire. In 1833, after Greece had finally gained its independence, Ludwig offered his seventeen year-old second son, Otto, as king to the newly independent state. Otto ruled from 1833 until 1862, when angry Greeks chased the Wittlesbach emperor out and ended so called "Bavarian absolutism." Still Otto, and the many Bavarian ministers that went with him, shaped the modern Greek state in the image of the Bavarian constitutional monarchy.[2] The colors of the Greek flag today are the colors of the House of Wittlesbach and Bavaria: white and blue.

This sense of sharing with the public is probably why Ludwig decided to open the Royal Court Brewery to the public, making it essentially a public house with chairs, benches and tables. In 1828 Ludwig I personally decreed that anyone could come to drink in the *Hofbräuhaus:*

. . . chairs and benches were placed around solid tables and every honest man could sit down in peace and enjoy his favorite drink drawn straight from the barrel. They came in their thousands until there was standing room only, and as King Ludwig I appeared amongst his people and wrote his name above the doors of the big hall, a roar of "God save the King" erupted throughout the hall, loud enough to make the barrels in the cellar shake. The *Hofbräuhaus* had become an acceptable member of society and the barrels had good reason to tremble.[3]

It was not long before the tourists showed up so that the reputation of the beer spread throughout the world. The clay beer steins in which the beer was served also began to spread around the world. The beer hall was strictly self-service. The customer went up to a rack where the beer mugs were stored, or found one on a table (if the stein's lid was left open it meant the mug was no longer in use). The next step was to find one of several troughs around the hall in which to wash the mug. After that one went to the cashier and paid for the mug of beer, then went to the barrels where the beer was dispensed and filled up. "The mugs are pushed along in Indian file under the flow, and are so deftly handled that the moment one is full the next one is shoved in its place, and so it sometimes happens that a barrel of several hundred quarts is emptied without once turning off the spigot." The lucky drinker would then elbow his way through the crowd to find a place to sit or make his way to the garden outside in order to enjoy the quenching brew.[4]

Even before Ludwig's reign, beer brewers began to expand their business by opening beer gardens to the public. Patrons could bring their own food or buy food in the garden, and sit and order as many beers as they could tolerate. When the brewers complained to the king that the practice of bringing one's own food was cutting into their profits, Ludwig effected a compromise: patrons could bring their own food but sit only at tables without table cloths. Tables with table cloths were reserved for patrons who were eating brewery food, or special guests (*stammgäste*), and these tables sometimes had waitress service.[5]

In the 1840s, known to historians of the period as the "Hungry Forties," food prices went up all over Europe. Bad weather caused bad harvests across the continent. In Ireland for example, a blight on potato crops led to some two million people dead from starvation. This was a period of intense competition for breweries. The number of large, corporate breweries declined throughout the nineteenth century due to fierce competition and take-overs. In 1790, Munich had about sixty large breweries, by 1819 there were thirty five and by 1865 Munich had fifteen large breweries. To be sure smaller breweries continued to proliferate so that there were about 5,400 breweries in the city and its immediate environs as late as 1882. Of all of these breweries the *Hofbräuhaus* remained the largest and most popular[6] because, as we shall see, *Hofbräuhaus* beer became the beer of the people in the nineteenth century. As beer and food prices continued to rise throughout the 1840s, revolution seemed certain. In May 1844 when the price of a liter of beer rose half a kreutzer, to over six kreutzer per liter, the first Munich "Beer War" broke out.

Korbinian Stieglmayer was the lowly soldier who, after consuming several liters of beer in the *Maderbräu* beer hall, was presented by a bill several kreutzers more than he anticipated. He complained out loud to the other patrons "26 kreutzer for four liters of beer that was poorly served." Apparently, no one had informed the patrons of the new prices. Stieglmayer, and the rest of the patrons began to smash up the hall. There was not a stein or window left in the place after the riots, that began on May 1, 1844 (the international day of the workers). After destroying the *Maderbräu,* the protesters then went throughout the city for days smashing up beer halls and the homes of local brewers until the brewers agreed to lower the price. A Paris daily reported that "Bavarians are a proud and peaceful people. But take away their beer, and they become 'wild revolutionaries.'"[7]

Thanks to Ludwig I, however, the *Hofbräuhaus* was spared the worst of the rioting. The riots on May 1 occurred on the same day as Albrecht of Austria married Hildegard, Princess of Bavaria. Therefore, the king ordered that the price increases be postponed until July. When in the fall protests began again, the King declared that the price of beer, at least in the *Hofbräuhaus,* would not rise above five kreutzers to "enable the working classes and the military to enjoy a healthy and inexpensive drink." Beer sales in the *Hofbräuhaus* then rose so quickly that the brewers could not keep up with demand.[8] Riots continued to flare up here and there in the next several months when the price increases could no longer be put off. The brewer at the *Lowenbräukeller* barely escaped with his life as he and his family escaped out the window of their house next to the brewery with a sheet, to avoid the rioting mobs. The master brewer of the *Pschorrbräu* and his family were less fortunate. They were held at bay while the angry mob threw everything they owned out the windows into the street and ransacked their home. The army had to be called in and several people were killed. To avoid even more destruction, the government eventually lowered the price of beer.[9]

In 1848–1849 yet another French Revolution broke out and revolution quickly spread to Germany and most of central Europe. The middle classes began to demand political reforms from an entrenched aristocracy, while the working classes demanded lower food prices, jobs, and fair pay. In the early years of his reign, Ludwig had opened just about everything he had to the public, including the Court's Brewery. He had also permitted limited freedom of the press and assembly, and appointed liberal ministers. He even allowed the formation of a customs union between Bavaria and Württemburg, the first free trade zone in the German confederation. After the French Revolution of 1830, however, and again in the 1840s, Ludwig tried to limit many of these freedoms, and the Bavarian population began to get angry. In March 1848, 10,000 angry intellectuals, students, and civil servants put forward a petition known as the "March Demands." They demanded, among other things, that the King's ministers be responsible to the parliament, that freedom of the press and the independence of the judiciary be guaranteed in a constitution, and that peoples' representatives be sent to the German parliament at Frankfurt, which was considering a constitution for a unified German nation.[10] In that same year Karl Marx and Friedrich Engels published their famous tract, *The Communist Manifesto*, which added to the revolutionary climate.

Then there was Lola Montez. This mysterious and alluring woman became the fuel to the revolutionary fire in 1848 Munich. Irish born (her real name was Eliza Gilbert) Lola had tramped her way across Europe as a "Spanish dancer" having affairs with the rich and famous all over the continent. Black hair, blue eyes, and the athletic body of a dancer, she reportedly lived with the composer Franz Liszt as his mistress before making her way to Munich in 1846. When the director of the Royal Theater refused permission for her to dance in Munich, Lola made a personal appeal to the king, presenting herself at the Residenz and demanding an audience with Ludwig I. When that failed she staked herself out in the imperial gardens in hopes of catching the monarch's attention. Unfortunately, aside from building, Ludwig's other hobby was pretty girls. When one of the guards described her to the king, Ludwig demanded to see her. Standing before the king, Ludwig was "bewitched." When he insisted that it was probably the supports in her dress that gave her such an incredible body, Lola reportedly ripped her bodice open showing the king her charms. Not only did she get royal permission to dance, Ludwig immediately fell in love with the Irish imposter.[11]

To put it mildly, Lola was trouble. Not long after the meeting with the king she was openly declaring that she was the king's mistress and this was, sadly, true. He bought her a house at number 7 *Barerstraße* which she demanded he renovate to her specifications. These included, among many other things, a fountain, bronze-gilded door knobs, and a mahogany hand-carved grand piano. The cost of the renovation came to over 40,000 florins, twenty per cent more than the king had agreed to spend.[12] Opposition to Lola, both in the government and in the streets of Munich, began to rise. Lola Montez became the proverbial "straw that broke the camel's back."

The court protested the amount of money the king spent on "his mistress." Gossip filled the beer halls and coffee houses about the king's romance. In fact, Lola was often to be found at the oaken tables of the *Hofbräuhaus*, surrounded by admirers and friends regaling them with stories of the king. She made no secret of the affair, and openly went about calling herself the king's mistress (much to the distress of the Queen). Ludwig demanded the cabinet approve his elevation of Lola to the nobility, making her the "Countess of Landsfeld, Baroness of Rosenthal." When the cabinet refused to grant her the Bavarian citizenship she required for the title, Ludwig dismissed the ministers and appointed a cabinet filled with the Spanish dancer's supporters. Riots broke out at the university between Lola's supporters and her enemies. When the king threatened to close the university, barricades went up and revolution followed.

Faced with a possible civil war in the streets very near the palace, the king reluctantly ordered Lola to leave the city. In March 1848 Ludwig withdrew all her titles and the Bavarian citizenship that the more pliant cabinet had granted. A few days later, having lost the confidence of his ministers and the respect of his subjects, Ludwig I abdicated the throne in favor of his son, who ruled as Maximilian II. Ludwig became the only German monarch to loose his throne during the turbulent "March Days" of 1848. The German Revolutions of 1848 ultimately came to naught. Even though the delegates at Frankfurt had worked out most of the details regarding the establishment of a unified German nation, Prussia's King, Friedrich-Wilhelm IV put the final nail in a united German's coffin. In 1849 the leaders of the Frankfurt Parliament offered a crown to the King of Prussia, asking him to become the King of Germany. They intended it as a complement, but he refused the crown. Insisting on his divine-right status, as a monarch who ruled by the grace of God, Friedrich-Wilhelm declared that he would not accept the crown from the "gutter." Bavaria then refused to ratify the constitution issued by the Frankfurt Parliament, essentially killing any hope for a unified German nation.[13]

Maximilian ruled until 1864. He quickly reinstated freedom of the press, guaranteed the independence of the judiciary, and introduced universal manhood suffrage. All of this had done little to quell the rising prices of food and beer. In Bavaria at least, beer had become a basic food staple to the German, especially for the farmers and working classes. Fluctuations in the price of beer meant less to eat. Moreover, since the government sometimes funded palaces and wars through manipulating the beer tax or beer prices, people knew that if beer prices went up, trouble was usually coming.[14] *Müncheners* seized on the situation to get cheaper beer prices. In October 1848 beer riots broke out again in Munich. Demonstrators marched through the streets demanding that the price of beer, which had once again risen to six kreutzers, be reduced to four. This time the military had to be called in and casualties resulted.[15]

During the reign of Maximilian II, Munich grew to over 100,000 people which presented a serious problem: sewage. City authorities had never planned a sewer system and the city stank. Moreover, disease plagued the city on more than one occasion in 1836 and again in 1850, killing over 3000 people. In 1854 the City Council hired Max von Pettenkofer, a physician and specialist in hygiene. Pettenkofer, along with the chief of city construction, Arnold Zenetti, established the first sewer system in Munich.[16]

During his reign, local brewers and pub owners complained to the king: they feared the royal competition from the *Hofbräuhaus*. Who could compete with the king? In 1852 the King approved the transfer of ownership of the *Hofbräuhaus* to the Bavarian state.[17] It now became the *Staatlisches Hofbräuhaus*. In the age of democratic revolution, the *Hofbräuhaus*, theoretically at least, belonged to the people. Almost everyone drank beer, and all social classes gathered in the beer hall. It was almost treasonous not to drink beer. Paul von Heyse, the famous Berlin writer transplanted to Bavaria in the 1850s, observed that the "humblest working man is aware that the highborn prince at court cannot get anything better to drink than he can." Class distinctions seemingly disappeared in the *Hofbräuhaus*. Visitors from other parts of Germany, and tourists from all over the world, received their first introduction to Bavarian culture by a visit to the famous beer hall. Thomas Wolf, the American writer visiting Munich in the 1930s, described best the electric atmosphere of the *Hofbräuhaus:*

> At night he walked the streets. He went into the crowded places. He sought the beer-fogged flash and roar, the enormous restaurants. He plunged into the roaring tumult of the Hofbrau Haus [sic], swung to the rhythm of that roaring life, breathed the air, felt the warmth, the surge, the powerful communion of those enormous bodies, gulped down from stone mugs liter after liter of the cold and powerful dark beer. He swung and swayed and roared and sang and shouted in the swaying mass . . . [18]

The *Hofbräuhaus* promoted liberty, freedom, and general good feeling, attributes that now came to characterize Munich. Maximilian sought to personify that liberty and freedom in a monument. In 1850 he commissioned the statue of "Bavaria" from Friedrich von Miller according to plans by Ludwig von Schwannthaler. The statue included a classical female holding aloft a laurel wreath in her right hand and a sword in her left. Next to her sat a lion. The statue, situated on the *Theresienwiese* where the Oktoberfest is held every year, became the symbol of Bavarian liberty. Cast in bronze, the statue remained the largest of its kind until the American Statue of Liberty was erected in New York Harbor in the 1880s.[19]

Maximilian encouraged all forms of folk culture, and during his reign Munich witnessed an increase of folk costume societies (*Trachtenvereine*) and shooting and hunting clubs (*Schutzenvereine*). In fact, Maximilian sponsored all sorts of tournaments and peoples' festivals to encourage the growth of these local and traditional societies. In 1855 he founded the Bavarian National Museum, and in 1862 the Museum for Folk Culture in Munich.[20] But Max did not ignore the liberal arts and sciences by any means. He encouraged scholars, scientists, and poets to take up residence in Munich and join the faculty at the university. Justus von Liebig, one of the founders of modern chemistry, and Paul von Heyse in literature, are just two who made Munich their personal and intellectual home in this period.

When Maximilian died in 1864, the "Dream King" Ludwig II ascended the throne. Few had ever seen the six foot, three inch crown prince but by all accounts he made a lasting impression on the population as he walked with his brother, Otto, in the funeral procession through Munich. Tall, fair skinned with curly black hair and piercing blue eyes, observers did not know quite what to make of him. Otto von Bismarck, the Prussian Chancellor, thought the eighteen year old prince looked too thin. But the public enthusiastically welcomed the new king to the capital city.[21] Ludwig II was less than two months into his reign when he sent a letter to one of Europe's most famous composers, Richard Wagner. In the letter, Ludwig begged Wagner to come to Bavaria to write his operas. Ludwig would pay all his debts, secure him a house, and pay him a generous salary. It took some time to locate the composer. In 1864 Wagner was in Stuttgart hiding from several creditors. He had been exiled from his native Saxony for his political views in 1848 (he supported a unified German republic), and had been on the run ever since. When finally reached, Wagner accepted the new king's invitation. Ludwig even bought him a house at 21 *Briennerstraße* in Munich, not far from the famous *Löwenbräukeller* beer hall and brewery on the *Stiglmaierplatz*.[22]

Ludwig was obsessed with the composer and his music and lavished large sums of money on him. Wagner became an item in the capital, and most people realized he had the ear and the protection of the king. Like Lola Montez twenty years before, however, the king's favorite took as much as he could. In the beer halls (where the best gossip and flavor of popular opinion was to be found) most felt that if the king wanted to keep a court composer instead of a private mistress around the palace, that was his business. But the king spent ever increasing sums of money to stage Wagner's productions, and bought the composer expensive gifts. Public opinion soon began to harden against the unwelcome Saxon musician. The money Ludwig was paying the composer was emptying the treasury and Wagner, again like Lola Montez, could not help but meddle in politics, even drawing up plans for a whole new Bavarian government. Soon, local *Müncheners* were calling the composer "Lolotte" (after Lola) and accusing him of being in a homosexual relationship with the monarch, who never married. Wagner had actually left his first wife for Cosima von Bülow, his conductor's wife. The king could barely tolerate this scandal and the citizens of Catholic Bavaria also found the situation distasteful. Homosexuality, however, was another matter. Ludwig could not tolerate the homosexual rumors: Wagner, like Lola twenty years before, had to go. In spring 1865 Ludwig ordered Wagner to leave the city.[23]

Still, the cord was not completely cut with Wagner. Originally, Ludwig had wanted to build a huge concert hall on the banks of the Isar River in Munich for the staging of Wagner's operas. He had even commissioned Gottfried Semper, the architect who designed the beautiful Semper Opera House in Dresden, to draw up plans for a Wagner Festival Hall. But the cabinet refused to approve the funds. Then Wagner had been forced to flee Munich. Wagner however began to fund a building of his own at Bayreuth near Nuremberg, but he quickly ran out of money. Ludwig again came to his rescue. The king had already partially funded the premiere of the Ring Cycle of operas at Bayreuth in 1871, having sent Wagner 75,000 Reichmarks. But in 1874, when it looked like Wagner's personal opera house would not be completed, the king sent him another 300,000 Reichmarks from his personal funds. The result is the impressive and famous "Wagner Festspielhaus" which hosts a Wagner festival every year.[24]

Ludwig II at first refused to support Otto von Bismarck in his attempt to unify all of the German Kingdoms (with the exception of Austria-Hungary) into a single empire (under Bismarck's plan, the King of Prussia, Ludwig's grandfather Wilhelm, would become the Emperor of Germany). Bavaria's ties with Austria-Hungary were far stronger than its ties with Protestant Prussia. Despite the family ties, Ludwig did not enjoy seeing the Habsburg Emperor humbled and humiliated before Prussian power. Yet Wagner had supported the idea of German unification for decades, and his ideas were not lost on the Bavarian monarch. Bismarck for his part, brought heavy pressure to bear on the "Dream King" including the promise of funds to complete the king's myriad building projects. In fall 1870 war broke out between France and Prussia (the Franco-Prussian War) and, after the spectacular victory of Prussian forces over the French at Sedan in 1871, there was simply no choice. Ludwig refused to attend the crowning ceremony for his grandfather in the Hall of Mirrors, January 18, 1871 in the famous Palace of Versailles, built by Louis XIV. However, Ludwig reluctantly sent a letter to Bismarck in France imploring his grandfather, Wilhelm I, to accept the Imperial Crown of a united Germany.[25] Germany had become a unified nation-state and Bavaria, after Prussia, became the largest single kingdom in this new German empire: the second German *"Reich."*

Integration into the new empire was not easy. Bavaria retained some special privileges but its army came under the command of Prussia in time of war. Further heightening the tension between Munich and Berlin was Bismarck's *"Kulturkampf,"* a campaign of intimidation and harassment aimed at suppressing the power of the Roman Catholic Church in Germany. Bismarck's policy was a reaction to the doctrine pronounced at the Vatican Council of 1870. That Council declared that when the Roman Pontiff spoke on matters of faith, he spoke and taught "infallibly." All Catholics were then bound by that teaching. Even some Catholics, including Ludwig, had a hard time with this doctrine. Ludwig interpreted it as a threat to his monarchial privilege and as an attempt by the church to undermine his subjects' loyalty and devotion to him. Bismarck saw it as an attempt by the Pope to undermine Catholic loyalties to the new German *Reich* headed, as it was, by a Protestant Emperor, Wilhelm I.[26]

Depressed at this turn of events, and the loss of his close association with Wagner, Ludwig retreated from what limited public life he enjoyed before 1871. Instead, he retreated into a dream world and began to build several glorious castles throughout southern Bavaria (hence the epithet "Dream King" for he spent most of his time dreaming of an imagined German medieval Wagnerian past). One such castle, *Neuschwanstein,* is well known to any visitor to Disney World since it served as the model for the castle in the Magic Kingdom. Begun in 1868, it was never truly completed but the outside and several interior rooms were finished by 1892. *Neuschwanstein* is completely decorated in Wagnerian scenes. *Linderhof* palace was also begun in 1868 and finished in 1874. *Herrenchiemsee,* begun in 1879 as a larger copy of the Palace of Versailles (with a hall of mirrors twice the size of Versailles), was also never finished.[27]

By the end of his life, Ludwig no longer made trips to the capital, claiming that "to live in this Munich would be my death." We now know that Ludwig was slowly going insane for the last fifteen years of his life. In fact, insanity ran in the Wittlesbach family. In the 19th century more than twenty members of the family had some form of mental disease. It was his limitless spending on the castles and his refusal to attend to matters of state that finally prompted the Bavarian government to seek his removal from the throne.[28]

In June of 1886 a Bavarian government commission declared Ludwig insane, arrested the king at *Neuschwanstein* castle, and brought him under house arrest to Starnberg. His jailer, and one of the officers sent to subdue him, was Lieutenant-Colonel Baron Charles von Washington, the king's Chamberlain and a distant relative of George Washington, the first President of the United States.[29] On a private walk with his doctor, Ludwig apparently killed himself by drowning in Lake Starnberg, or drowned while trying to escape. His doctor, trying to save him, died as well. Ludwig's uncle Luitpold ruled as Prinz-Regent in place of Ludwig's brother, the completely mad Otto. Otto was by this time so insane that the family confined him to *Hohenschwangau* palace.

During Ludwig's reign, Germany had been unified into one country and this boded well for *Hofbräuhaus* beer. Soon it was readily available in

Stuttgart, Hamburg, and even Berlin, and quickly acquired a reputation as the best beer in the nation.[30] Around this time, the beer began to acquire an international reputation as well. In 1878, the U.S. Civil War General and President Ulysees S. Grant visited Munich. The American Consul intended to show the General all of the attractions of the city, but especially the churches and museums. Grant would have none of it. Instead he expressed an interest in visiting the "Court Brewery."

> When we drew up to that noble building and entered the yard and tried to wedge our way through the crowd of people standing elbow to elbow, and each armed with a quart pot in his hand, and heard the hum of thousands of voices and saw the happy expressions of gusto in the faces of the drinkers, I noticed for the first and only time during his visit an approach to a smile on the General's staid countenance.

When Grant and the Consul finally got their beer and made their way out to the garden, the General "put his quart inside of him without winking. He only stopped once in the middle to take a breath and to remark 'Ah, this is excellent beer!' When I asked him if he would like to have another go, he said 'My mercy, I could hardly get that down!' " But he had not yet had enough. That same evening in September 1878, the General visited the beer hall again on his own. This time he sat at a table and waited to be served by a waitress, something locals and tourists rarely did. Grant caused an even bigger stir when he gave the waitress a two mark (roughly 50 cents) tip.[31] Americans loved the atmosphere in the city. Mark Twain lived in Munich around this time, at *Nymphenburgerstraße* 45. While in Munich he wrote *A Tramp Abroad* and finished his masterpiece, *The Adventures of Huckleberry Finn*.[32]

Soon the famous "HB" with crown symbol would be world famous. In 1879 that symbol, the official symbol of the Court Brewery, was registered in Munich and Berlin as the trademark of *Hofbräuhaus* beer. Meanwhile, demand had risen so rapidly that by the 1890s, the facilities on the *Platzl* were simply no longer big enough to brew the amount of beer needed for domestic, not to mention foreign consumption. Therefore, in 1896 the actual brewing facility relocated to the *Hofbräukeller* annex on the *Innere-Wiener Straße*. On May 22, 1896 the last beer was brewed at the *Platzl* location.[33] On August 10, 1896 the new, larger brewery began its operations. The *Hofbräuhaus am Platzl* now underwent an extensive renovation to become the "most famous beer hall in the world."

4. The "Golden Years" of Munich: 1897–1918

On May 22, 1896 the last barrel of beer was brewed in the *Hofbräuhaus am Platzl*. Throughout the summer and winter, and on into 1897, the *Hofbräuhaus* underwent a complete transformation, turning it at last into the "most famous beer hall in the world." These are the years known as the "golden years" of the city. Corresponding roughly to the years when Prince Regent Luitpold governed in place of the mad King Otto (Ludwig II's younger brother) Munich became an industrial city, and was no longer merely a provincial art city on the banks of the Isar. The population nearly tripled and the demand for beer, the Bavarian national drink, skyrocketed. In this period all the major breweries transformed themselves into huge "beer temples" and restaurants.

In the summer of 1896 all brewing operations were moved to the *Hofbräuhaus Keller* on the Innerer-Wiener Straße in the Au district, on the east side of town. Opened as early as 1836 as an annex to the main operation on the *Platzl*, the *Hofbräuhaus Keller* served as the main brewery for *Hofbräuhaus* beer until 1988. The architectural firm of Heilmann and Littmann was employed to totally transformed the building on the *Platzl* into a large beer hall and restaurant. The former brewery was not just renovated, it was expanded. The state bought up neighboring houses and incorporated them into the plans for the new building. The total renovation, which lasted less than a year, cost RM 819,000.[1] The new restaurant opened on February 9, 1897.

At least twenty large beer halls were built or renovated in Munich in the period between 1880 and 1902 (not to mention the many smaller ones attached to smaller breweries). Beer consumption tripled, and beer had replaced schnapps as the average drink of choice. Since beer was important, and the beer hall such an important gathering place, the beer hall itself had to reflect that importance. Expansion could be afforded by the large increase in business, a growing export business, and the transformation of many of the larger breweries into joint-stock companies. Most of the large beer halls then being reconstructed in the city were modeled on the "New Bavarian Renaissance" style architecture: ornate gabled exteriors, large vaulted rooms, and even small cozier rooms inside to accommodate almost every taste.[2] Heilmann and Littman also remodeled the famous Orlando House on the *Platzl* (home of the former sixteenth century court composer Orlando di Lasso). The *Hofbräuhaus* and Orlando House renovations were so successful, that the firm also received commissions to remodel other beer halls and restaurants throughout the city. The Prince Regent took a personal interest in the renovations, and insisted on approving the architectural plans himself. Heilmann and Littmann also renovated the famous *Mäthaserbräu,* operated by the *Löwenbräu* brewery which until the 1990s was the largest beer hall in the world.[3]

Between 1890 and 1910 several breweries expanded into large restaurants/beer halls: *Hofbräuhaus* 1896–1897; *Maderbräu/Weissesbräuhaus* 1903–1904; *Pschorrbräu* 1895–1896; *Augustinerbräu* (*Neuhauserstraße*) 1897–1898. Common to all the beer halls was some form of large banquet room or "Festsaal" which accommodated two thousand or more people, usually on the top floor. Generally, on the ground floor was the "*Schwemme*" a large room open to the public for drinking. There was music usually in the garden, sometimes in the *schwemme,* and various other forms of entertainment in other parts of the restaurant. By the turn of the century the *Hofbräuhaus* had the largest *schwemme* and one of the more beautiful beer gardens.[4]

By the 1890s the beer hall, and beer itself, came to be identified with Bavaria and Germanic culture. Aside from the unique Bavarian dialect and the *lederhosen,* the beer hall became a unique, hallowed cultural institution, a national symbol. Since the 1840s beer had been the drink of choice for the radical student fraternities (*Burschenschaften*) that had often championed the cause of democracy and liberalism. To them, beer was seen as an ancient beverage, peculiarly German. It was also the common man's drink so that beer came to be seen as a nationalist, even democratic beverage. The beer hall, then, came to be seen as peculiarly "German" and a unique Bavarian institution to which anyone could belong. Even women came to the beer hall without escort, and all classes mixed together to drink, talk, and make merry[5]. Bavarian "*gemütlichkeit*" was born in the beer hall.

To satisfy the demands of the large crowds, two innovations were made to the *Hofbräuhaus* that have endured to the present day. Under the direction of Josef Widtmann, *Hofbräuhaus* manager from 1897–1906, the kitchen was kept open for warm food until 11:00 P.M. to compete with other restaurants in the city. Another innovation was the addition of a corps of *Hofbräuhaus kellnerinnen:* waitresses. In addition to serving food, waitresses would also obtain beer for patrons, often carrying five or even ten liter mugs to a table at a time. Generally speaking, self service for beer, once the norm, was now reserved only to very special *stammgäste*.[6]

By the 1890s Munich had become a center of science and technology. Therefore, in 1906, Oskar von Miller a pioneer in electrical engineering, and others founded the German Museum (*Deutsches Museum*). The museum was established to display the many scientific and technological inventions of the city, Bavaria and Germany. The German Emperor, Kaiser Wilhelm II, visited Munich in 1906 to lay the foundation stone for the museum, built on an island in the middle of the Isar river. One of the machines that could have been displayed there was the first usable "ice machine" or refrigerator invented by Carl von Linde in 1874. By the 1890s, refrigeration had become commonplace. Beer could be stored for longer periods of time and a cellar was no longer necessary. Intense competition during this period of rapid industrialization led to the consolidation of smaller breweries with larger ones. Still, beer production doubled and the quality improved.[7]

Competition, and the increasing economic strains leading to World War One, led to an actual decline in the number of breweries in the city. In 1889 there were twelve large breweries and by 1914 there were nine within the city. Today there are six (really four) large breweries in Munich. *Hofbräuhaus* is probably the most famous. *Augustinerbräu*, brewed by Augustinian monks since 1328, secularized in 1803, and since 1829 owned and operated as a private brewery. *Augustinerbräu*, brewed since the nineteenth century on the *Landsbergerstraße*, is viewed by many today as Munich's best tasting beer. *Löwenbräu* is probably Bavaria's most internationally known beer. Brewed since at least 1397, it was only in 1883 that the brewery's owner, Georg Brey, moved the brewery operation to the *Stieglmaierplatz* and built a magnificent beer hall to go with it. Then there is *Hacker-Pschorr Bräu* brewing since 1793; *Paulanerbräu*, also founded by monks in 1629; and lastly *Spatenbräu* that dates to 1397. These six breweries ruled the beer scene in Munich in the nineteenth and early twentieth centuries. They are the only breweries allowed to sell beer at the famous Oktoberfest festival held every year in Munich. In the late nineteenth century, export business grew substantially. By 1906 there was even a *Hofbräuhaus* in New York City and several other places served *Hofbräuhaus* beer, such as Luchow's on 14th Street.[8]

The Industrial Revolution had forced the closing of many small shops and ended the careers of hundreds of craftsman in the big cities. In Munich, at least until the end of the nineteenth century, one remained: Clock Maker Falk (*"Uhrmacher Falk"*). Falk had a clock shop right near the Karl's Gate on the west side of the old city, and the clock maker had a very delicate palate for beer. Every day he would visit the local beer halls to test their brews. When they saw him coming, servers would immediately bring a fresh liter of beer. If he downed it in three gulps, he liked it; if he did not like the beer, he pushed the liter away after only one gulp and left the establishment. Brewer's feared this latter action, because Falk would then return to his shop and post his beer ratings outside the shop. Local *Müncheners,* and those passing through the gate into the city, would check Falk's ratings before deciding on a place to drink. Even the local press relied on Falk's beer reviews.[9]

Rapid industrialization led to mass emigration. As early as 1847 a "National Association for German Emigration" was founded at Munich and in other cities, but it was only with rapid industrialization in the 1870s-1890s that emigration began to explode. Between 1871 and 1885 1 1/2 million Germans left Germany for the Americas. About 95% of these emigrants went to the USA,[10] demonstrating that the "Golden Years" weren't all that golden for the laboring classes. Rapid industrialization created social tensions and conflicts throughout Germany that the war would later unleash. As industrialization expanded, the need for workers increased. Many of the workers that found employment in Munich were Germans from other parts of the country, but many others were foreigners from other parts of Europe, especially eastern Europe. In addition, the social problems associated with a rapidly industrializing city became wide spread: homelessness, begging, robbery, drunkenness, and prostitution increased.[11] For all these reasons, the Social Democratic Party, a political movement dedicated to alleviating the afflictions of the working class, emerged in Munich and throughout Germany in the 1870s, 1880s and 1890s. George von Vollmar was the leader of Munich's Social Democrats until after World War I. By 1912 the "SPD" (*Sozialistischer Partei Deutschlands*) was one of the largest parties in the Bavarian *Lantag.*[12]

One of the stronger voices in the working class movement in Munich in the 1890s was the voice of the beer hall waitress. The working conditions of waitresses in the *Hofbräuhaus* were especially bad. Often, toothpicks, salt and pepper, even the clay beer steins used by the patrons, and the beer, were paid for by the waitresses themselves. The waitresses were not paid a salary: they earned whatever the customer left as a tip. Some waitresses worked all day, twelve hours, in order to make adequate money. In addition, beer-waitress was sometimes the only employment a woman could find. Therefore, they had to be very careful not to offend the employer or the customer, even having to endure unwanted sexual advances and other forms of harassment. They could risk their tip, the little money they made, or forfeit their job. In 1900 the beer waitresses of Munich founded the *Münchener Kellnerinnenvereins* (the Munich Waitresses Association). In 1902 waitresses held a demonstration at the "Kollergarten" beer hall demanding better wages. Then, in 1905 the *Hofbräuhaus* waitresses went on strike. They demanded wages, better working conditions and health care.[13]

As the population of Munich increased, and the working class population rose, there was an increasing demand for public forms of entertainment. Much of that entertainment was supplied in the beer hall, but in 1874 a theater-restaurant opened just across from the *Hofbräuhaus*. In 1906, after a thorough renovation and expansion, the restaurant opened as the "*Platzl Bühne*" ("The Stage on the Platzl"). The *Platzl Bühne* afforded food and traditional Bavarian entertainment including genuine Bavarian folk music performed by the *D' Dachauer* along with regular *Schuplattler* dancing.[14] Before movie theaters and dance halls became the norm, the beer hall and dinner-theaters such as the *Platzl Bühne* became the favorite place for popular entertainment. The *Platzl* area then became one of Munich's entertainment districts. This was the period, before sound films and movies, when the "*Volksinger*" ("Folk Singer," roughly the equivalent of a cabaret artist) reigned supreme in Munich. The *Volksänger* were performers that sang folk songs and performed short musical sketches and even small plays, satirical skits, and comedy routines. They wrote their own material and performed to suit the tastes of their audience, peppering their work with an abundance of Bavarian one-liners and dialect that only true natives could understand. The *Hofbräuhaus* was a familiar place to many of these performers, as was the *Platzl Bühne*. Two of Munich's best known satirists were Karl Valentin and Weiß Ferdl.[15]

One of Weiß Ferdl's most famous acts was called "North and South in the Hofbräuhaus" which he performed with Paul Westermeier. In the sketch, a Prussian sits with a Bavarian in the *Hofbräuhaus* and they discuss the differences between the two regions in Germany. The Prussian, in clear high German, insists that they, too, have a "*Hofbräuhaus*" in Berlin. "No way" says the Bavarian (Ferdl) in perfect Bavarian dialect. "You may have music, even a beer hall, but not the beer" insisting that there is just no way to replicate the *Hofbräuhaus* without the beer, which can only be made in Bavaria. As the sketch progresses the argument gets even more heated. The two even argue over how to tell the correct time until a chorus of "*Ein Prosit der Gemütlichkeit*" drowns out the two of them. The skit implies that even strong regional differences are overcome in the *Hofbräuhaus* or that Bavarian culture conquers all.[16]

In addition to the fun and entertainment provided, the beer hall became the place for meetings. Political and social groups often held meetings in the beer hall. In fact, between 1870 and 1910 the number of official clubs (*Vereine*) in Munich rose from 310 to 4,500. Many of these clubs reserved a table in their favorite beer hall to meet every week or every month (only a lucky few met every day!). This led to the rise of the *Stammtisch* or the table reserved for customers or groups who met on a regular basis. Only members of that group could sit at that table at the time the table was reserved. Ornate wooden or metal signs were placed on or above these tables, signifying that the group theoretically owned the table. Members had a right to sit at that table anytime they visited the beer hall. Usually, they were established by local groups who applied to the beer hall directly. Friendship societies, bowling clubs, even cat lover societies had their own reserved table. Some drinkers even brought their own personal steins to drink from and some beer halls provided cupboards where these could be stored from meeting to meeting.[17]

All classes of people sat together in the newly expanded *Hofbräuhaus* and the other establishments popping up throughout the city. While all of the patrons came for the beer, many also came for the food. Still, patrons could bring their own food if they so desired and many did bring cheese, ham, sausages, and bread. Sometimes they shared with other patrons or guests at their table, enhancing the *gemütlichkeit* experience. By royal decree, the beer in the *Hofbräuhaus* was always a few pfennigs cheaper than other breweries. Therefore, the *Hofbräuhaus* became one of the more popular (and most crowded) beer halls in the city.[18]

Paul von Heyse, the famous author and Nobel prize winner, testified to the egalitarian atmosphere of the *Hofbräuhaus*. "The lowliest worker is confident that even the highest born prince can't obtain a better drink than he . . ." Heyse even wrote a poem to the *Hofbräuhaus:* "Ode to Hofbräuhaus Bock Beer":

> Here one finds on fraternal benches
> Great and small in familiar mix
> the servant not far from his stabled horses
> the bureaucrats from their imperial offices.
> Porter, Professor, Pharmacist and Student
> [Hofbräuhaus beer washes] away the barriers that divide them.[19]

Some scholars have referred to the *stammtisch* as the "cradle of democracy" in Germany since the tables were not organized by any national organization or controlled by any outside forces. Whereas in the country side there was a hierarchy among *stammtisch* visitors (farmers usually sat with farmers, carpenters with carpenters, etc.), in the city such a hierarchy was impossible. This was especially true in the *Hofbräuhaus* where hundreds of visitors streamed through the doors every day. Paul von Heyse observed that such an eclectic mix of people and classes (such as one found in the *Hofbräuhaus)* would never occur in Berlin. They were drawn there not only by the excellent beer, but the fun and a chance to socialize. In fact, because of the jovial and stress-free atmosphere, some Munich psychiatrists recommended that their patients visit the local beer hall at least once a week.[20] The *stammtisch* fostered the "live and let live" *gemütlich* atmosphere. It served as a social safety valve where people could get together to complain about politics, local or national officials, the church, and over-powerful bureaucrats. Of course the government watched the *stammtisch* and the beer hall as places of opposition, but the beer hall posed less of a threat than the government feared, at least until after 1918.[21]

The *Hofbräuhaus* became the place to meet the average Bavarian. Ludwig Thoma, another famous Bavarian author memorialized the "average Joe" Bavarian in a famous work called the "Angel from Munich (*"Der Münchener im Himmel"*). The "Angel from Munich" tells the story of a porter from Munich's Central Train station, Porter number 172: Alois Hingerl. One day Hingerl dies at his post and is taken up into heaven. Hingerl doesn't like heaven, especially worshiping and singing all day long. In fact, he is so miserable in heaven, and his singing is so bad, that God Himself has to intervene. Called before the Almighty, Hingerl declares "I don't like to sing and I don't like manna! I like beer!" "Ah!" God replies, "an Angel from Munich!" He made Hingerl an "Angelic Messenger" figuring that if He let Hingerl fly to Munich once or twice a week, that would satisfy the former porter. Soon God gave him his first assignment: deliver an important message to the Bavarian Government. Hingerl flew as fast as he could: but to the *Hofbräuhaus*. He found his *stammtisch* and ordered a beer, then another, then another. "He sits there to this day" the story concludes, "which is why the Bavarian government to this day operates without any divine advice."[22] The "Angel from Munich" and Alois Hingerl has become the unofficial symbol of the city, after the (official) little benedictine monk with the radish and beer stein.

Beer consumption reached record levels by the turn of the century as the city's population grew. The numbers demonstrate the total triumph of beer culture in the rapidly expanding city of Munich. By 1900, Mathias Pschorr the owner of the *Hackerbräu* was the largest tax payer in the city, and of the sixteen richest people in Munich, eleven of them were brewers. The first motor car made its debut in 1888. Made by the Benz company of Mannheim, the car went 16 miles per hour. By 1900 there were roughly 54 cars licensed in Munich. The first electric street cars appeared in 1895 and by 1900 most of the streets, at least in the main city, were paved.[23]

And the city shone brightly. By the 1890s electric lights had been added to many of Munich's major thoroughfares. Street lamps and torches had been used to light the streets of the city since at least 1729. By 1848, gas lanterns replaced the torches. Then, on December 1, 1893 the city replaced many of the gas lanterns with electric light. By 1920 electric lanterns outnumbered gas lamps in the city. Albert Einstein, the famous physicist and author of Relativity Theory, may have become Munich's most famous scientist had it not been for electricity. Einstein's father and uncle owned an electrical company in Munich. Their customers included most of Schwabing and the *Schottenhamel* beer concern at the Oktoberfest. The *Schottenhamel* tent was the first to use electric lights rather than gas lanterns at the Oktoberfest, and Albert Einstein himself helped install the wiring. In 1894 however, Einstein's father lost a bid to electrify the city to the Siemen's company, so he moved the family to Italy. Albert Einstein eventually took up residence in Zurich, Switzerland and published many of his famous scientific theories from that city.[24]

In the years just before the war, the beer hall became the chief meeting place for political groups and agitators. Munich attracted more than its share of revolutionaries. Two of the most famous were Vladimir Lenin and Adolf Hitler. Vladimir Lenin, the leader of the Bolshevik Revolution in Russia in 1917, lived as an exile in Munich in the early twentieth century and was often a visitor to the *Hofbräuhaus*. He and his wife, Krupskaya lived at *Kaiserstrasse* 14 under the name "Meyer" between 1900 and 1913. It was from Munich that Lenin and fellow exiled Russian Marxists published the journal "Iskra" ("the Spark") which was then smuggled into Russia. Here Lenin wrote his famous revolutionary book "What is to be Done?" Some scholars have claimed that Lenin planned the Russian Revolution of 1917 while living in Munich. Not only did Lenin and his wife enjoy the beer and the *gemütlichkeit* the *Hofbräuhaus* afforded, Lenin also noted that the German characters "H" and "B" when translated into Russian characters actually stand for "N" and "W" which are the abbreviation for the Russian phrase "Peoples' Will." What Lenin thought of the royal crown over the letters which represent the trademark symbol of the *Hofbräuhaus* is not recorded.[25] The fact that a Lenin and a Hitler could both live in Munich testifies to the fertile political atmosphere of the city in the years before World War I. Thomas Mann, one of Germany's most famous writers, also lived in Munich before World War I and often praised its "popular character," its "*Volkstümlichkeit.*" Mann described Munich as a "rich topsoil of which the most peculiar, tender, and audacious things, and sometimes exotic plants, could thrive under truly favorable conditions."[26]

Artists flocked to the city. Franz von Lenbach was one of the most famous artists living in the city at the time. Lenbach painted the portraits of the European rich and famous including German Chancellor Otto von Bismarck, and Pope Leo XIII. In fact a "Lenbach Circle" emerged around the artist as other aspiring artists sought to copy the master. One such copier was the "*Hofbräuhaus Lenbach*" Franz Mandlinger. Mandlinger spent up to twelve hours a day in the *Hofbräuhaus* drawing customers portraits or painting their likenesses for fifty pfennigs or a liter of beer, and he subsisted on this and any scraps of food he could find in the *Hofbräuhaus*. Because he looked a little like the master Franz von Lenbach, customers referred to him as the "*Hofbräuhaus* Lenbach."[27]

The city attracted other famous artists, writers, poets, and scholars that took up residence in Munich. Henrik Ibsen, the famous playwright lived in Munich in the 1870s and 1880s and wrote many of his famous plays in the city including *Hedda Gabler.* Ibsen insisted that there were really only two cities in Europe worth living in: Rome and Munich. The famous author Franz Wedekind sat in the *schwemme* of the *Hofbräuhaus* for hours day after day observing people and discovering characters for his work.[28]

Still there were some who chose not to join the Lenbach circle and instead founded their own artistic movement. "Seceding" from the Lenbach circle and his style of art, Fritz von Uhde founded the Secessionist Movement which spearheaded the emerging impressionist school of art. The Secessionist artists rejected Lenbach's landscapes and portraits. Uhde and another famous Munich artist, Franz Stuck, set up camp in Schwabing, a rural area just north of Munich's old city, and this quickly became the high-brow, Bohemian-artist quarter of the city.[29] Soon not only artists, but poets, writers, and musicians began to flock to Schwabing. Many of them were from Germany, but many from outside Germany and Eastern Europe moved to Schwabing as well. In fact, native *Müncheners* referred to Schwabing inhabitants as the "Slawiner" or the Slavs. Old *Müncheners* viewed them as foreign and different. Schwabingers, in their cosmopolitan chic, patronized cafes and rejected the beer hall culture of the old city. Vasily Kandinsky (1866–1944) lived in Schwabing in this period and founded the "Blaue Reiter" artistic movement. In addition to pioneering abstract art, he wrote many influential books and essays including the influential essay "Concerning the Spiritual in Art" in 1912.[30]

In the 1890s, two important magazines were published from Munich: *Jugend* (Youth) and *Simplicissimus* (Simplicity). Both magazines offered a critical and satiric review of art and culture in Germany and Europe. The artistic production associated with Schwabing in this period is sometimes referred to as "*Jugendstil*" (Youthful or Young Style) which is similar to "Art Nouveau." Ludwig Thoma was the editor of *Simplicissimus,* Henrik Ibsen and Thomas and Heinrich Mann regularly contributed to the journal. The Mann brothers, Ibsen and others moved to Munich in this period because of the artistic vitality and the freedom they found in Schwabing, which is also where the university is located.[31] Before Berlin in the 1920s, Munich possessed the liveliest and most exciting cabaret scene in all of Germany. In what would become known as the "Simplicissimus Affair," Wedekind spent seven months in jail for a satirical piece he wrote regarding the Kaiser's trip to Palestine in 1899. Censors confiscated all copies of the magazine in which the article appeared and charged Wedekind with "*Lese Majesty.*" On his release, Franz Wedekind joined Ludwig Thoma and others in "Die Elf Schar-frichter" ("The Eleven Executioners") a cabaret troupe that performed reg-ularly in the Café Stephanie, one of Schwabing's most popular cabarets. Decorated as a medieval court of justice complete with skeletons and execu-tion devices, the "Executioners" made fun of local and national politics, and international affairs. The actors would sometimes give two performances. Wedekind, for example, would often present one version of his act to the cen-sors, then present a more lively (and controversial) version for his audience once on stage.[32]

As more Jews, especially those of east European extraction, began to take up residence in the city, anti-Semitism became more pronounced. Bavarian Jews had been granted full legal status in the middle of the nineteenth cen-tury and Munich's Jews were well integrated into the community. Foreign Jews, and foreigners generally (though not tourists) had a hard time in the city, especially if they could not speak German. A writer at the time remarked that "like the Chinese to California came the Jews to Munich: diligent, fru-gal, numerous, and thoroughly hated."[33]

On June 28, 1914 Munich's Golden Years, indeed the "Belle Epoch" in Europe, came to an abrupt end. On this date the Serbian terrorist, Gavrilo Princep, shot and killed the Austro-Hungarian Archduke, Franz Ferdinand, and his wife while riding in a carriage in Sarajevo. The assassination was the spark that ignited the conflagration known as the "Great War": World War I. The war ushered in social and political changes that began even before the outbreak of war in 1914. Prince Regent Luitpold, who served as the regent for Ludwig II's even madder brother Otto since 1886, (and who had stepped down in 1912) finally died in December 1914. Luitpold's son Ludwig served first as Regent, then after pleas from the public, as King Ludwig III (officially deposing the mad Otto in November 1913). The insane ex-King Otto died during the war, in 1916. Paul von Heyse, one of the city's greatest authors died on the dawn of war, August 2, 1914. Food had become a problem even before the war. The rapid increase in population throughout the nineteenth century led to increased demands for food and lodging so that the prices for these items continued to climb right up to 1914. Rising food price rises had already out paced wage increases by 1912 in Bavaria, and in north Germany prices were rising even faster. Local "land barons" were not above manipu-lating supply and demand and prices.[34]

Many welcomed the war as a way to break out of what they saw as social, economic, political and international pressures. Thomas Mann was one among hundreds of those who celebrated the advent of war in 1914. "War! It meant a cleansing, a liberation, . . . And an extraordinary sense of hope . . ." The Social Democrats, up until 1914 strongly pacifist, voted to support the war effort in July 1914. The German Kaiser, pleased that even the Socialists supported the war, declared that he no longer recognized political parties. "I recognize only Germans!" he announced on August 4, 1914, in what became known as the "*Burgfrieden*" or "the Fortress Peace." All Germans, it seemed, were united around the flag and the Kaiser in support of the war effort. The general population was so infected with war fever, that many advocated changing the name of the "English Garden" to something a little more Teutonic like the "German Garden."[35] Adolf Hitler himself joined the revelers on the Odeonsplatz to welcome the announcement of war in 1914. Few realized that the war would represent a watershed: nothing would be the same in Munich, Germany or Europe when the guns finally went silent.

Hitler's attraction for the city in the years before the war lay in its artistic caliber. Hitler fled Vienna in 1913 after being thoroughly rejected by the artistic community (he twice failed to gain entrance to art school while living in the city). To have Hitler tell it, he fell instantly in love with Munich, calling it "a German City."[36]

> What a difference from Vienna. I grew sick to my stomach when I even thought back on this Babylon of races . . . But most of all I was attracted by this wonderful marriage of primordial power and fine artistic mood, this single line from the *Hofbräuhaus* to the *Odeon*, from the October Festival to the *Pinakothek*, etc.[37]

Hitler moved to Schwabing, *Schliessheimerstrasse* 34, in 1913 and declared his profession "Architectural Painter from Vienna" to his landlady, Frau Popp. He earned a modest living by painting postcards and water colors of all the major buildings of Munich, the *Frauendom*, the *Feldherrnhalle*, the *Alte Hof* and last but not least, the *Hofbräuhaus*[38] and selling these paintings around the city, much like he had done in Vienna.

Hitler's early experience in Munich seems to have been a solitary one. He seldom talked about his family in Vienna, and never mentioned that he had any friends, nor was he ever seen with any. Hitler seems to have had no male friends in Munich, and there is no evidence that he ever had female companionship during this period. Except for a roommate for the first nine months, there is no evidence that he had any personal relationships in Munich before World War I.[39] There is also no evidence that Hitler attempted to make any friends in Munich or took advantage of its many cultural institutions. According to his landlady, Hitler did nothing all day but paint. And when he was not painting, he was out on the town trying to sell his paintings. One of the best places to sell his work was the *Löwengarten*, the shady little beer garden in the courtyard of the *Hofbräuhaus*. He sold primarily to tourists, but sometimes even locals bought his watercolors. In the summer of 1913, Dr. Hans Schirmer observed Hitler trying desperately to sell his paintings in the crowded beer garden, without much success:

Around ten o'clock I saw him again and observed that he had still not sold any of his pictures . . . I asked him if he was trying to sell these paintings to which he replied a very hearty "yes." The price was RM 5.

After a night of drinking, the good doctor had only three *Reichmarks* left, gave it to Hitler and promised the rest if Hitler would come to his home the following day, deliver the painting, and collect the other two *Reichmarks*. Eager to clinch the sale, Hitler insisted that he take the painting right then, and he promised to come by and get the rest of the money the next day. The picture was titled "Der Abend" ("Evening"). With the three RM, Hitler "went over to the buffet and bought two pair of Vienna sausage and bread, but had no beer." The next day when Hitler came to Dr. Schirmer's to collect the other two RM he persuaded the doctor to buy a few more paintings. It is clear that Hitler usually sold paintings through word of mouth and that after he sold one painting to someone, he usually got commissions for more. A jeweler, Paul Kerber, bought 21 paintings from Hitler in 1913–1914.[40]

By the end of 1913, Hitler was well known in Munich art stores, and known to many art dealers so that he generally received very good commissions for work and made pretty good earnings.[41] Dr. Josef Schell bought several pictures from the future *Führer* in Munich in this period. Later, after World War I, when Hitler was beginning his political career, Dr. Schell went to the *Hofbräuhaus* to see if Hitler the politician was the same Hitler he had bought a painting from years before. It was, in fact, the same Hitler. The painting he had bought then for RM 20 was a portrayal of the building in which he now stood: the *Hofbräuhaus am Platzl*.[42] When war broke out in August 1914, Hitler volunteered for military service with the Royal Bavarian Army and served with distinction as a dispatch runner. He attained the rank of corporal, was wounded twice, and earned the Iron Cross first and second class. Still, even in the army he seems to have made few if any friends.

At the outset of war in 1914, the British imposed a total marine blockade, effectively closing off the North Sea trade routes with Germany. The food situation throughout Germany deteriorated drastically the longer the war endured. And whereas most people in Europe believed that war would last only a few months, by the summer of 1915, a year after the first shots were fired, there was still no end in sight. In 1914 King Ludwig III banned the Oktoberfest because many believed it improper to spend money on "frivolities" during the "present political situation." During the war years, beer was heavily watered down and many *Müncheners* blamed Ludwig III on the grounds that he allowed the export of Bavarian hops to the north, where it was turned into schnapps. Ernst Toller, later one of the leaders of Munich's socialist revolution in 1918, argued that "because the Prussian swine didn't mind bad beer, the Bavarians also had to drink dishwater!"[43] By June 1915, there was already a serious beer shortage in Munich because much of the material for brewing had been confiscated by the military. Most beer gardens were forced to close at 7:00PM because of a beer shortage.[44] In December the brewers demanded a price increase for beer but this was disallowed by the Bavarian authorities, fearing riots. Already in 1914, the government ordered that beer production be cut to 60% of the prewar amount. By 1916 the authorities ordered beer production cut again to 45% of the prewar levels. Bock beer brewing was stopped entirely.[45]

Food riots became common by 1916. In one episode a crowd of about twenty-five thousand *Müncheners* took part and caused serious damage to the Town Hall and several neighboring houses.[46] The beer halls of Munich experienced their first economic collapse during the war since the raw materials needed to make beer became harder to find. As the war dragged on, the government confiscated brewery machinery, much of which was made of steel, iron, and copper, for the war effort to make weapons. The government confiscated and melted down organ pipes and bells from Bavarian churches for military use. In the age of "Total War" nothing was sacred. The export beer business all but dried up as foreign markets refused to buy German products.[47]

The city was forced to establish soup kitchens and "cheap eating houses" so that the poorer citizens could get a sustaining meal. But even the more prominent citizens were hard-pressed to find a decent meal. Oswald Spengler, the famous historian and author, wrote to a friend in 1916 that he was living on "a 1/5 [kilo] Limburger [cheese] and 1/4 [kilo] bad sausage a week. Recently, in the Pschorr Brewery Restaurant the only 'meat' dish they had was a piece of cod . . ."[48] As the war dragged on, the situation got even worse. Undernourished children from the cities were sent to the countryside where they might be better fed. Figures by Professor Friedrich von Müller, claimed that men under fifty years had lost 9.3% of body weight by 1917; over fifty lost 12 %; women had lost 6.7% of their body weight by 1917, over fifty, 10%. In the countryside, there was a gain in weight since 1914. The blockade hit the cities hardest. A United States government report showed that by 1918 tuberculosis and stomach troubles affecting most of the population had increased due to lack of food and undernourishment.[49]

The police were constantly searching for those hoarding food and material used for heating and lighting, and constantly fighting the black market. In 1916, a Munich engineer invented a machine that could "powder" food for storage. By June 1918 Bavarians were reduced to eating fake ("*ersatz*") food such as powdered milk, fruit, and eggs and the government was forced to order "meatless weeks." Famine had begun to plague the Tyrol region of Austria and all-out food riots seized Salzburg by September 1918. Fake beer, powdered eggs, and turnips were the only basic staples by war's end.[50] By fall 1918, Germany and Bavaria were on the brink of collapse.

And yet war came to Munich in other ways as well. In November 1916 a French pilot, Captain de Beauchamp, flew his plane some 435 miles from France to Munich and dropped six bombs on Munich's Central Train Station. The bombing was in retaliation for the German destruction of Amiens early in the war. Flying at sixty miles an hour at about 35,000 feet, Beauchamp swooped down over Munich around noon and bombarded the train station by surprise. Some months before, he had bombed the Kaiser's headquarters at Mezeleres-Charleville, forcing the Kaiser and his staff to flee.[51]

By November 1918, Munich had become one huge mass of peace protests. Rainer Maria Rilke, another of Munich's famous literati, noted that many of the protests demanding an end to the war and more food took place in the open spaces of the city. Gradually, peace protests began to be held in the large beer halls as well.[52] Some of the loudest protests came from Munich's women. Since the late nineteenth century Munich had been one of the most vital centers of the women's movement in Germany. Led by Anita Augspurg and Lida Heymann, women had been demanding equal rights and the right to vote even before the war. They now lent their voices to the budding peace movement, demanding that women stop working in the ammunition factories, military hospitals, and refrain from making military uniforms. Some 9000 women were employed in factories throughout the city during the war years. About 188,000 Bavarians died in World War I; 13,000 of these were from Munich.[53]

The war ushered in turbulent times for Germany and Europe. Even the beer hall, including the *Hofbräuhaus,* became caught up in the changes wrought by four years of war, and the technological and political changes that followed in its wake. After the war, movie theaters, dance halls and night clubs became commonplace and the beer hall lost its place as the center of popular entertainment in the city. Increasingly beer halls became the center of political developments, renting their large rooms to political parties for their meetings.[54] The *Hofbräuhaus* was an important gathering space for many political parties after 1918. But no party, and no political leader, would make better use of the facility than Adolf Hitler and his *National Socialist German Worker's Party.* By 1918, Munich's Golden Years had ended.

**Figure 1. The Towers of Munich (from left to right):
St. Peter's Church, Holy Ghost Church, the Twin Towers
of the Cathedral, and Town Hall Tower with *Glockenspiel*.**

**Figure 2. The *Hofbräuhaus am Platzl*,
"the most famous beer hall in the world."**

**Figure 3. The famous Town Hall tower with Glockenspiel Clock.
The figures move to reenact the wedding of Wilhelm V,
Duke of Bavaria and the founder of the *Hofbräuhaus*.**

Figure 4. Bavaria, the symbol of Bavarian liberty. Situated on Munich's Oktoberfest grounds, it was the largest bronze statue of its kind until the Statue of Liberty was erected in New York Harbor.

Figure 5. Oktoberfest! The largest beer drinking party in the world. Held each year on Munich's Theresienwiese, the festival commemorates the wedding of Crown Prince Ludwig who ruled as Ludwig I. (1825–1848).

Figure 6. The "HB" symbol with Crown, one of the most internationally recognized trademarks in the world.

5. Chaos Theory: Revolutionary Munich

In the period before World War I, the beer hall had become synonymous with Bavarian culture. Munich, the city of "good feeling" had changed dramatically in the four years since the outbreak of war. First of all, it was only during the war that Munich became a truly industrial city. The longer the war dragged on, the more armaments factories that sprang up throughout the city. The working class increased while food became scarce. Three quarters of a million Germans died from starvation during the war due to the lack of food caused, in part, by the British blockade. Revolution, political turmoil, and class conflict erupted throughout the city as the "Great War" drew to a close. After 1918, the beer hall found itself directly at the center of Bavarian revolutionary politics. Political power had shifted, in a sense, from the parliament and palace, to the beer hall and the streets: from the monarchy to the mob. The *Hofbräuhaus* and all of the major beer halls in Munich, became political battle stations in the turbulent years between the wars.

By summer and fall 1918 strikes and food riots were common in Munich as they were throughout Germany. By November the political situation deteriorated as the military situation collapsed. In November, peace riots and rallies erupted in all the beer halls of Munich. Then, on November 7, workers and soldiers meeting in the *Mathäser* beer hall (Munich's largest beer hall at the time) declared themselves a "Workers' and Soldiers' Soviet." That same day, during a peace demonstration on Munich's famous *Theresienwiese* Kurt Eisner, leader of the Bavarian Independent Socialists, proclaimed a socialist republic and demanded the immediate abdication of the king. Eisner insisted that all political power in Bavaria rested in the hands of the workers and soldiers' councils. The king learned of all these events while taking his daily walk in the English Gardens.[1] At 10:30 P.M. that evening Eisner proclaimed himself "Provisional Prime Minister" in the name of the council of workers and soldiers. By Friday (8 November 1918) the "revolution" was complete. The "Free State of Bavaria" was a republic. The *coup d' etat* in Munich had been completely bloodless,[2] at least at the beginning. By war's end, the Wittelsbach family had fallen out of favor with the citizens of Munich. The king's brother, Leopold and the Crown Prince Rupprecht, both served in the army, and too close to Prussian interests for Bavarian tastes. Thus, the Wittelsbach family got the blame for all the war's misfortunes. By November, fearing for his life and his family's security, Ludwig III fled the city the same evening of Eisner's *coup*. Faced with the *fait accompli*, Ludwig proceeded first to Austria, and then on to Hungary where he died in 1921.[3] The longest reigning ruling house in Europe had vanished over night. Meanwhile in Munich, public buildings, monuments, and churches bore placards announcing the new regime.

Once in power, the revolutionary government proved thoroughly incapable of governing. Class warfare had been unleashed in the city, and many feared that a Bolshevik revolution similar to Lenin's Russian Revolution would soon follow. There was still a serious lack of food and housing, and the hundreds of returning (and armed!) soldiers made the situation dangerous. During the few months of his government Eisner found it increasingly difficult to forge a working coalition or find popular support for his programs. Part of the reason for his failure was that, ironically, Eisner was not a Bavarian: he was actually a Jewish former journalist from Berlin. Throughout his regime he suffered repeated defeats at the polls, ridicule in the press, even harassment in cabinet meetings. Eisner's popularity dwindled rapidly during the three short months of his ministry.[4] In a scene that would repeat itself throughout Germany in the 1920s, a right wing nationalist, Count Arco Valley, shot and killed Eisner on February 21, 1919 on his way to parliament to submit his resignation. On March 7, the Majority Socialist leader Adolf Hoffmann attempted to form a coalition government[5] but this government lasted little more than a month. The paralysis of the economy, lack of support from most other political parties, and the conflicting aims of the revolutionary leadership quickly led to the Hoffmann government's demise.[6]

On Palm Sunday, April 1919, the Bolsheviks came. "Orthodox" Communists supported by Vladimir Lenin's revolutionary government, seized power in Munich. Hoffmann and his government fled the city for Bamberg. The leadership of the new "Bavarian Soviet Republic" fell to three Russians: Eugene Levine, Victor Axelrod, and Max Levien, all sent to Munich by the Communist Party of Berlin. Their arrival in Munich brought the class war in the city to a head. A reign of terror began, mitigated only slightly by inefficiency and confusion. The new regime closed schools, banks, newspaper offices, the National Theater, and imposed a curfew in the beer halls. The revolutionary leadership called for a general strike, released criminals from prison, and burned police files.[7]

To enforce its measures, the regime established a Soviet style "Red Army." Privates received twenty-five *Reichmarks* a day; officers received one-hundred *Reichmarks* a day, and bonuses. One historian has called the Bavarian Red Army "probably the best paid army in history." Families of Red Army soldiers received free living quarters, and the soldiers received free liquor and prostitutes.[8] To pay for all these "luxuries," the triumvirate demanded all citizens turn over their cash in exchange for credit slips. When this failed to raise the required sum, the regime confiscated all private safes and safe deposit boxes in the city. Finally, the regime threatened to seize the vaults of Munich's major banks, but only panic ensued. When terror failed to raise enough money, the regime ordered money printed,[9] which aggravated the already severe inflation of the currency. As the Communist grip on Munich tightened, the exiled Hoffmann government requested troops from Berlin to help regain control of the city. Berlin sent the Ritter von Epp *Freikorps* battalion which first encircled and blockaded Munich, and began to slowly take control of the city.[10]

Opposition to the Bolshevik leadership came not only from the Bavarian middle classes and the aristocracy: it came from the revolutionaries themselves. As the blockade around Munich tightened, panic seized the regime. On April 26 the Supreme Soviet, known as the "*Hofbräuhaus Parliament*" because it met daily in Munich's most famous beer hall, convened in emergency session. The delegates complained that seizing vaults and deposit boxes amounted to "political theft" and they accused the Russians of paying too little attention to particular Bavarian circumstances. Ernst Toller, speaking for the Bavarian socialists, insisted that "We Bavarians are not Russians!" Instead of a "Bavarian Revolution of Love," as Toller, a poet and playwright described it, the Bavarian revolution had degenerated into a Teutonic nightmare. On April 27, the *Hofbräuhaus* Parliament passed a no confidence resolution against the Russian leadership, and demanded their resignation and 35 other members of the regime.[11]

Bolsheviks do not resign. Instead, the leadership became even more radical. In response to the increasing disorder, the Soviet leadership seized all food supplies in Munich, in part to avoid hoarding, but also to ensure that the Red Army remained well fed (and therefore ready to maintain them in power). The Red Army now entered and searched private homes and shops at will, taking whatever they pleased.[12] Opposition to the looting and lawlessness, and the bolshevik regime, increased. Moreover, while economic conditions in the city became ever more desperate, the revolutionary leadership continued to live very well. *Müncheners* knew about the sex parties, the drinking, and luxuries the leadership hoarded for themselves in the Communist headquarters, the former Wittelsbach Palace.[13] Bavarians of all classes began to resent the fact that the top revolutionary leadership was Russian and Jewish, foreigners getting rich off of the misfortunes of local *Müncheners*.

Müncheners began to equate Socialism and Communism, and therefore the Socialist Revolution, with thievery, lawlessness, and anarchy. Werner Heisenberg, the renowned physicist, later insisted that, "Pillage and robbery, of which I myself once had direct experience, made the expression 'Räterepublik' [Soviet Republic] appear to be a synonym for lawless conditions." According to his own account, Adolf Hitler narrowly escaped arrest by revolutionary authorities in Munich at this time, fighting them off with a pistol.[14] Weiss Ferdl, one of Munich's more famous contemporary satirists, summarized revolutionary events this way:

> Freedom and justice rule over the country,
> Take whatever you like from the stuffed-up bunch
> Whatever's not nailed down belongs to us—
> that's for sure!

Some scholars have argued that one of the reasons Pope Pius XII became such a fervent anti-communist was because of his experience with the Bolshevik regime in Bavaria in 1919. Pope Pius XII, formerly Cardinal Eugenio Pacelli, served as Papal Nuncio at Munich during the revolutionary period.[15]

When the defense of the Soviet state appeared hopeless, terror broke out across the city. The regime ordered the execution of twenty prominent "bourgeois" hostages held at Munich's famous *Luitpoldgymnasium*. This is actually something Lenin had recommended in a series of revolutionary guidelines he sent the Russians on April 29. However, Bavarians in the Red Army refused to carry out the murder decree. Therefore the Bolshevik leadership ordered Russian soldiers sent to Munich by the "Third Communist International" to perform the executions. The murders so outraged the citizens of Munich, that they formed local self defense groups (*"Einwohnerwahren"* or citizens militias), attacked Communist authorities and soldiers, and aided the *Freikorps* in their conquest of the city.[16]

Berlin's suppression of the Bavarian Soviet was even more bloody than the revolution. The "white" forces that ultimately crushed the Munich Soviet murdered indiscriminately throughout the city as their hold on Munich tightened. In one episode in March, the *Hofbräuhauskeller* on the Innerer-Wiener Strasse became the scene of a brutal reprisal. The Freikorps Battalion Lutzow arrested twelve people from Perlach whom they termed "Spartacists" (communist revolutionaries). They were shot in the beer hall's garden without trial or any type of investigation.[17] Scenes like this were repeated throughout the city for weeks afterward.

There is no question that the seeds of Hitler's later political attractiveness, at least in Bavaria, were sown during the Revolution of 1919. At the beginning, Bavarians supported the revolutionary leadership in their efforts to secure peace, restore order and promote economic recovery. The Bolshevik interlude ended that era of good feeling. The Russians destroyed what little support Socialism may have had among the middle classes in Bavaria up until that time. The revolution had become, in the words of a contemporary observer, "one huge sin against the Bavarian spirit."[18] This was the climate in Munich when Hitler became politically active in the years just after World War I.

Despite his claims to the contrary, Hitler too probably supported the Socialist cause in this period. If not an active revolutionary, he certainly had socialist leanings. Recently, historians have discovered a film of Hitler, dressed as a lance corporal wearing a red armband, marching in the funeral procession of Kurt Eisner in February 1919.[19] The fact that he was elected the political leader of his demobilization battalion in February 1919, suggests to some scholars that Hitler had to have expressed socialist leanings.[20] Hitler's "world view," both as a fanatical right wing nationalist and as a fervent anti-Semite, most likely took shape in Munich after World War I, and not during his days in Vienna before 1913 as he later claimed in *Mein Kampf*. Hitler's transformation from "left" to "right" was not that uncommon. Scholars have noted that many of the most revolutionary elements of the 1918 Bavarian Revolution later became some of Hitler's most loyal followers. The war and revolution had changed Munich and the political climate, that city of good feeling, would not be the same for decades. Political radicalization, and the latent anti-Semitism prevalent in Munich before World War I, broke out into the open after the war.[21]

Any hope that the events of 1918–1919 would somehow bring about a new era of peace, democracy, and freedom in Germany faded when the Allies announced the conditions of the Versailles Treaty in June 1919. Above all, with Article 238 (the "Guilt Clause"), the victors laid all guilt for the war on Germany, and compelled the new government to pay war damages and reparations to the victors. Failure to sign the Treaty, or to pay the reparations, would result in military occupation by the victors. In addition to thievery, terror, economic chaos, and political instability, now military defeat and national humiliation were added to the list of the new Weimar Republic's accomplishments.

The Versailles Treaty is what united all Germans in their anger, regardless of political persuasion: everyone loathed the "Dictated Peace" (*Diktat*). Had it not been for the infamous Versailles Treaty, the world might not have ever heard the name Adolf Hitler. By all accounts, Hitler enjoyed his military service and might very well have remained in the army and pursued a modest career. But the treaty limited the German Army to no more than 100,000 men. Hitler, and thousands of soldiers like him, would eventually have to be dismissed. Had the army bothered to enforce a decree by the Bavarian War Ministry of August 1914, which barred Austrians from conscription into the Bavarian army, Hitler might have been forced to return to Austria in 1914 and never heard from again.[22] This would not be the first time Hitler was able to avoid the law, fall through the cracks, and remain in Germany.

Still, the army found a use for the artist-soldier that shaped his future political career. After the Soviet Revolution, Munich came under the indirect military rule of a Bavarian *Reichswehr* division *"Gruppenkommando Nr. 4."* The *Gruppenkommando* (GRUKO for short) sought out veterans who could be used to spy on political parties or revolutionary groups and help foster a nationalist education among the troops returning to civilian life. GRUKO recruited Adolf Hitler and sent him to the University of Munich for political training. These were the days when Hitler's political views solidified. Once trained, army officials then sent Hitler out to speak to the troops about the dangers of Marxism and Jewish revolutionaries. He was also sent to observe the many political groups sprouting up all over Munich. In September 1919, Hitler was sent to observe a small group calling itself "The German Workers' Party." Meeting in a back room of the *Sterneckerbräu,* a small beer hall not far from the city center, Hitler apparently took over the meeting. He thought that the party was "dull" and "insignificant" and was almost about to leave, when someone in the meeting suggested that Bavaria separate from the Reich and form a south German state with Austria. Hitler then went on the attack:

> At this point I could not help demanding the floor and giving the learned gentleman my opinion on this point - with the result that the previous speaker, even before I was finished, left the hall like a wet poodle . . . As I spoke, the audience had listened with astonished faces, and only as I was beginning to say goodnight to the assemblage and go away did a man come leaping after me, introduce himself . . . and press a little booklet into my hand, apparently a political pamphlet, with the request that I read it.

Hitler apparently liked what he read, because shortly after this he joined the group as member number 555.[23]

He then set out to turn the party into a mass movement. The party adopted the black swastika, on a white disk, imposed on a red flag as its emblem. Hitler then began to draw up a list of principles for his new "movement." The first mass meeting of the German Worker's Party organized by Hitler took place at the *Hofbräuhaus* on 16 October 1919. Seventy people attended, which represented a substantial increase in its membership. According to reports, the meeting enhanced Hitler's reputation as a powerful speaker.[24] A month later another mass meeting was held at the *Hofbräuhaus,* and this time the German Workers' Party attracted their largest crowd ever: 111 people.[25] Hitler decided to quit the army and work for the party full-time. He had found his true love: politics.

Hitler's new *National Socialist German Workers' Party* was born in the *Hofbräuhaus*. One of the most important meetings for the young party took place on February 24, 1920 in the Festival Hall of the *Hofbräuhaus* with some 2,000 people in attendance. Hitler was not the main speaker that evening. The star attraction was a well known right-wing physician named Johann Dingfelder. Most of the people assembled in the *Festsaal* that evening were from leftist radical parties.[26] Once Hitler began to speak, some people in the crowd threw their beer steins at him. Ducking the flying mugs, Hitler paused while loyalists in the crowd cleared out the protesters with their own beer steins, whips, and rubber truncheons.[27] Hitler spoke only briefly that evening, attacking democracy, the regime, Jews, and the Versailles Treaty. Then he briefly announced the "Twenty-Five Points" of his party, which became the official party program of the newly constituted *National Socialist German Worker's Party* (NSDAP in German, or "Nazi"). This meeting marks the true beginning of the Nazi Party.

Despite the flying mugs, Hitler was elated. In *Mein Kampf* he declared how happy he was that these mass meetings attracted all the right people: communists and socialists from whom he hoped to recruit many followers.

> At 7:15 I entered the *Festsaal* of the *Hofbräuhaus* on the Platzl in Munich, and my heart nearly burst for joy. The gigantic hall—for at that time it still seemed to me gigantic—was overcrowded with people shoulder to shoulder, a mass numbering almost 2000 people. And above all—those people to whom we wanted to appeal had come. Far more than half the hall seemed to be occupied by communists and independents.[28]

The meeting in the *Festsaal*, however, is significant for it marks a distinctive Hitler characteristic. At its founding, the NSDAP was merely one racist-nationalist party among many in Munich and throughout Germany at the time. Hitler however sought to distinguish the new party from the others by making it a mass revolutionary movement. His strategy was to hold meetings in the largest beer halls or meeting places in the city, and attract as many people as possible to hear his message. If fights broke out, all the better, as that attracted more people (and the newspapers) to the meetings. That would bring the free publicity Hitler craved for the still struggling movement. In fact, since he encouraged confrontation, in 1920 the party created a "Hall Protection Unit" made up of loyal supporters. This unit became the "Gymnastic and Sport Division" of the NSDAP in 1921, and this organization eventually morphed into the SA: the *Stürm Abteilung* or Storm Troops.[29]

They were characterized by their brown uniforms, black jack-boots, swastika armbands, and thoroughly nasty disposition.

By late 1920 Hitler was the main attraction at these mass meetings. Most people in Munich, possibly even throughout Bavaria, could recognize him by sight, while many had heard him speak at one time or another. In 1920 alone Hitler appeared as main speaker at least twenty-seven times, and at least seven more times as commentator or discussion leader. He must have spoken to thousands in 1920, picking up recruits here and there at each meeting. At one meeting in the *Hofbräuhaus* in May 1920, Hitler announced that force was a justifiable means for the party to achieve its political ends.[30] Nothing he said was unique. Most of Hitler's ideas can be easily traced back to the Pan-German movements and *Völkisch* (racist) ideology of nineteenth century Germany and Austria. It was the way he spoke, combined with the peculiar economic and political situation in Germany after World War I, that made both the message and the messenger popular.[31]

Little more than a year later, on July 29, 1921 the party became the personal tool of its master. There had been talk within the party that it might be a good idea to merge with either the German Socialist Party (a right wing party not to be confused with SPD: Socialist Party of Germany) or the *Deutsche Werkgemeinschaft* in order to improve membership and attract a broader audience. This would have threatened Hitler's leadership role in the movement. Had the proposed merger gone through, Hitler would have become a small fish in a very large pond. This he could not tolerate. He resigned the party and refused to come back unless all talk of the merger ceased and he was invested with "dictatorial powers."[32]

At a special meeting in the *Hofbräuhaus,* with five-hundred, fifty-four members of the Munich branch in attendance, the membership invested Hitler with full dictatorial powers as leader of the NSDAP. It can be argued, therefore, that Hitler's first true "seizure of power" actually occurred in the *Hofbräuhaus* on that hot July evening in 1921. From this point forward the main goal of the party was to gain political power for Adolf Hitler. The message and the mass rallies stayed pretty much the same. Hitler seemed to champion the concerns of the little man: the lost war and the Versailles Treaty, the influx of so many eastern Jews and other immigrants, the turmoil of the Marxist Soviet of 1919, the poor economy, the increasing unemployment, the growing poverty of the working and middle class, and the inflation. In short, Hitler complained about all the stuff the average German complained about in their local beer hall.[33]

Some of the Nazis' earliest formative experiences occurred in the famous beer hall and not in the street battles that would be common later. Some of Hitler's earliest anti-Semitic pronouncements were made from the rostrum in the *Hofbräuhaus.* At a meeting on August 13, 1921 he is recorded as calling for the "removal of the Jews from the midst of our people."[34] This speech, titled "Why We Are Anti-Semites" was delivered in the *Festsaal* of the *Hof-bräuhaus* to an audience of about 2000 people. The speech was interrupted by applause 58 times and lasted two hours.[35] At a another meeting, on November 4, 1921 the Storm Troopers, which had by now reached a strength of 300, rose to defend their leader when he came under attacks by leftists in the crowd. Hitler paused his speech as his Storm Troopers threw themselves "like wolves in packs of eight or ten again and again on their ene-mies, and little by little thrashed them out of the hall." After this "*Battle of the Hofbräuhaus*," Hitler informed his SA men that "We have won a major battle. You have survived a baptism by fire, despite being outnumbered." Hitler was very pleased that the local population was calling the Storm Troopers a "raw and brutal bunch who were afraid of nothing."[36] By 1921 it was clear that the Nazi Party was not simply one racist party among dozens; it was rather a terrorist organization every bit as dangerous as the Communists.

Other nationalist organizations felt the *Führer's* wrath as well, not just the Communists. Having conquered the Nazi party, Hitler now wanted to conquer the right-wing political scene as well. He used his storm troopers to break up the meetings of rival political parties in his attempt to make the NSDAP the only nationalist, right-wing organization in Munich. For exam-ple, in September 1921 Hitler and his men stormed into the *Löwenbräukeller* to disrupt a meeting of the "*Bayernbund*" a conservative federation that advocated, among other things, a return of the monarchy. Shouting "Hitler" over and over again in chorus, fights eventually erupted, the police had to be called, and the meeting was cancelled. The leader of the *Bayernbund* pressed charges and Hitler went to jail for this: less than two months in *Stadelheim* prison for disturbing the peace.[37]

The NSDAP was not the only party to invade the *Hofbräuhaus* either. On November 9, 1922 the United Patriotic Organizations of Bavaria held a mass assembly in the famous *Festsaal* of the *Hofbräuhaus*. Hitler, it is reported, was received with loud "heils," evidence that his fame was increas-ing.[38] By the late fall of 1922 Hitler was being compared with that other nationalist agitator who had successfully gained power in Italy: Benito Mus-solini. (In October 1922 Mussolini marched on Rome with his "Black Shirts." Rather than crush the former journalist and his militant band of Fas-cists and risk a civil war, and to avoid a communist grab for power, the king appointed "*Il Duce*" Prime Minister of Italy). In a speech in a packed *Fest-saal*, Hermann Esser declared that "Germany's Mussolini is called Adolf Hitler!"[39]

As fall 1922 ran its course, it looked like Hitler might very well end up copying Mussolini and gaining political power in Germany. There were already rumors in 1922 that Hitler might be planning a *putsch,*[40] something that looked increasingly more likely as the economic and political situation worsened. Early in 1923, when Germany failed to make its first reparations payment to the Allies, French and Belgian troops occupied the Rhineland. In protest, the German government called for a campaign of passive resistance in the occupied territories. In response, Hitler and the Nazis held their first "Reich Party Rally" in Munich January 27–29. Party faithful filled all of the major beer halls in Munich and Hitler made the rounds, preaching at each one. On the night of January 27, Hitler made some twelve speeches. At the *Hofbräuhaus* he was greeted as "a savior" and at the *Löwenbräukeller* he received a hero's welcome. Here Hitler also used the outstretched right-arm salute (which Mussolini and his Black Shirts also used) and by 1926 this became the common salute for the party.[41]

In March, French occupation troops killed thirteen and wounded forty-one workers at the Krupp factory in Essen. In October, Communist revolts erupted in many German cities. Inflation continued to rise to dangerous levels since the government insisted on printing more and more money to cover its bills. By November, one US dollar bought 4,2 trillion *Reichmarks.* Before the war, one US dollar bought just four *Reichmarks.*[42] The severity of the inflation can be demonstrated by beer prices. For example, in 1916 one *maß* (liter) of *Hofbräuhaus* beer cost 34 pfennigs (100 pfennigs = 1 *Reichmark*); by November 19, 1923 that same liter of beer cost 260 billion *Reichmarks!*[43] By November 26 1923, two weeks after the failed Hitler-Putsch, one liter of *Hofbräuhaus* beer cost 266 billion marks![44] In response to all these events, the Bavarian government planned to hold a mass meeting on November 8 in the *Bürgerbräukeller,* one of Munich's largest beer halls on the east side of town.

During the famous "Beer Hall Putsch" all of Munich's major beer halls became, in one form or another, armed revolutionary fortresses. Whereas most of the *putsch* saga unfolded at the *Bürgerbräukeller,* the *Löwenbräukeller* on the west side of town also played a role in the events of November 8, 1923. The beer hall on the *Stieglmaierplatz* was filled with drunken, rowdy Brown Shirts awaiting their *Führer's* order to "march." Ernst Röhm, leader of the SA, interrupted the boisterous drinking to give patriotic speeches whenever the brass band took a break. By 11:00 P.M. that evening, all of Munich's beer halls were packed with Brown Shirts or members of other right-wing organizations waiting for something to happen. The police knew that something was afoot: they knew about the large numbers of SA men at the *Löwenbräukeller.* They knew too of a "*Völkische Rechtsblock*" (Right-Wing Racist Block) meeting at the *Hofbräuhaus.* And the police knew of the meeting held by Gustav von Kahr and the Bavarian government at the *Bürgerbräukeller.* What the police did not realize is that some of these groups were armed, and had hidden weapons and ammunition at or near these beer halls, waiting for the command to action.[45]

Hitler decided that now was the time to act. He planned to march into the *Bürgerbräukeller* with his Brown Shirts and arrest von Kahr and the rest of the government. Then, after seizing political power in Bavaria, he would march to Berlin and establish a nationalist dictatorship, gaining popular support for his revolution along the way. In his efforts he was joined by General Erich Ludendorff, one of Germany's supreme commanders in World War I, and Hermann Göring, a member of the "Red Baron's" flying squadron in the Great War. At 8:30 P.M. on November 8 Hitler marched into the large cavernous beer hall, jumped onto a table, and fired a shot from his browning revolver into the ceiling. "I declare the Bavarian government deposed! The Reich government is deposed! A provisional Reich government is being formed. The Police and *Reichswehr* have joined our banner, the swastika banner, which at this moment is flying above the barracks and police stations of this city." But he was lying. The army had not joined his revolution nor was the swastika flag flying over the army barracks of the city. Von Kahr and his ministers, unsure of the situation outside the beer hall, decided to "play along with the comedy" until they could find an opportunity to escape. When they were later released, they quickly called for reinforcements to retake control of the city and suppress the *putsch*.[46]

The next day, the "Hitler *putsch*" ended in gunfire on the Odeonsplatz, just north of city hall. Hitler, and most of the leaders of the attempted *coup d' etat*, were arrested. Revelers in the *Hofbräuhaus* learned of the collapse of the *putsch* from those fleeing the scene trying to hide from the police. During the trial which followed, the famous standup Weiss Ferdl provided entertainment for the crowd at the *Hofbräuhaus* singing his own commentary about the trial, and expressing many of his fellow countrymen's feelings. "German men stand today at the bar of the court. Tell me, what have they done wrong? Can it really be a crime to try and save one's fatherland from disgrace and despair?" According to the "Law for the Protection of the Republic" passed in 1922, foreigners convicted of political crimes in the Republic were supposed to be deported. Hitler should have been deported to Austria. However, the prosecutor in the case allowed Hitler to make a three hour speech in his own defense. The judge in the case seemed to agree with the sentiments expressed in Weiss Ferdl's little song, and probably with Hitler's "little" speech. In the verdict the judge refused to apply the "Law for the Protection of the Republic" to Hitler. The judge reasoned that the law did not apply "to a man who thought and felt so like a German."[47]

Sentenced to five years in prison, Hitler was out by Christmas 1924 for "good behavior." The years after the *putsch* witnessed an economic stability known as the "Golden Years" of the Weimar Republic. Once Hitler got out of prison he started slowly to rebuild his political base. Still, with the economy stable, and the Berlin government gaining some international recognition for Germany (For example, the Allies finally allowed Germany to join the League of Nations in 1924), party membership stayed pretty-much flat. Hitler announced the reestablishment of the NSDAP in the *Bürgerbräu* beer hall on February 27, 1925. He might have announced the reconstitution of the party on February 24, the actual birthday of the party. But February 24, 1925 was *"Faschingsdienstag:"* Mardi Gras. No beer hall was going to cancel the day's festivities to accommodate a political meeting. Three-thousand people attended, two-thousand had to be turned away. Total NSDAP membership in Munich stayed at roughly four-thousand (4,945)[48] until the calamity known as the "Great Depression" threw German politics into chaos once again.

Radical parties of the right and left attracted members only during bad economic times. The Great Depression (1929), which represented a worldwide economic collapse, thrust Germany back to the days of 1923. The beer halls again became filled with revolutionaries of all political stripes calling for the end of democracy and right-wing (or left-wing) dictatorship of the people. Hitler once again, had his chance. Rather than ban these political parties (and violate the constitution's guarantees of free speech), the Bavarian Minister-President Heinrich Held prohibited the beer halls where the Nazis and Communists met from serving alcohol and food. The government hoped that Bavarians would not attend meetings where they could not eat or drink. The next year, Held's government banned the wearing of uniforms by political parties. The Nazis cheated the beer ban by drinking their fill before big political meetings. They avoided the uniform ban by marching around in simple white shirts with black neck ties.[49]

Throughout 1929 and into 1930, as unemployment and homelessness raged across Germany, applications for party membership increased rapidly. The Brown Shirts, or SA became a sort of welfare organization, offering enticements to membership such as food and clothing, lodging, even money. Between 1931 and 1932 SA membership rose from 77,000 to 471,000 members. Party workers went into the soup kitchens, unemployment offices, and factories to recruit members. By this time the NSDAP was one of the largest political movements in Germany, second only to the Socialist Party (the Communists were third).[50]

In Berlin, the German President, Paul von Hindenburg, faced a dilemma: no one political party could gain enough seats in the *Reichstag* to form a proper government. Hindenburg, the aging Great War icon, appointed several chancellors throughout 1931–1932 in an attempt to avoid a Socialist coalition government and keep the conservative barons in power. But the conservative prime ministers Hindenburg appointed could not muster enough popular support to form a stable enough government. And Hindenburg despised Hitler, "the vulgar little corporal." Yet, by 1933 Hindenburg faced almost the same situation as the Italian king faced in 1922: appoint the Fascist or face a possible Communist revolution, civil war, or a complete social collapse. Germany's fate hung in the balance. One observer described the old general as a "Zero paving the way for a Nero."[51] Hitler's *"satyricon"* was about to begin.

6. *The "New Order"*

Adolf Hitler did not "seize" political power in 1933, nor did he ever win a free election. Hitler obtained political power on January 30, 1933 as the result of a back-room political deal. With no end in sight to the economic chaos and the political confusion, the aging President Hindenburg used Article 48 of the constitution to appoint Hitler chancellor. In a deal worked out between former chancellor Franz von Papen and Hindenburg, Hitler would become Chancellor, and von Papen Vice-Chancellor. Through this deal they hoped to block a possible Socialist-left coalition and maintain their own political influence. With Hindenburg as President, and Papen as Vice Chancellor, they believed they had the Austrian corporal "boxed in." Von Papen declared that in a few months "we will have pushed Hitler so far into a corner that he'll squeak!"[1]

Hitler, of course, had other ideas. He realized that the key to political control was not only from the top down, but from the bottom up. Despite the torchlight parade through Berlin on that cold January night, the party was not in power at the regional or local levels, at least not in any organized way. The months after January 1933 witnessed the real revolution: the illegal seizure of power by the party in the towns and villages throughout Germany. Hitler was not "boxed in."

On 28 February 1933 the *Reichstag* building in Berlin burned down. The regime declared that the fire was the opening act of a Communist revolution. The police arrested several known Communists in addition to Marinus van der Lubbe, the young Dutch construction worker caught after the fire. Claiming a "national emergency," the government suspended several articles of the Weimar Constitution. Alarmed and unsure of themselves, Hindenburg and von Papen consented to these measures. Known as the *Reichstag* Fire Decree ("Law for the Protection of the People and the State"), the law suspended the right of due process, protection from arbitrary arrest and search, and freedoms of speech and assembly. At the same time, the government reorganized the court system to enforce the new decrees.[2] The regime now arrested hundreds of Communists and Socialists, and anyone else they feared. The trial of van der Lubbe uncovered no "national conspiracy" but the regime got what it wanted: suspension of civil liberties. This was the opening act in the creation of the National Socialist terror state; Germany now lived under a permanent "state of emergency."

On March 9, 1933 Brown Shirts stormed and occupied Munich's Town Hall, terrorizing and beating anyone who got in their way. Through threats and intimidation, they forced the Lord Mayor of Munich, Dr. Karl Scharnagl, to resign and replaced him with Karl Fiehler, a Nazi. The Nazi administration then placed Bavaria under the control of Ritter von Epp as "State Commissar." Later, in 1935 the regime abolished the "Free State of Bavaria" and reorganized all Germany into "*Gaue*" or districts. Each "*Gau*" had a "*Gauleiter*" that reported directly to Hitler. Hitler appointed Adolf Wagner *Gauleiter* of Bavaria. Similar "revolutions" happened throughout the Reich in 1933 and 1934, while Hindenburg and von Papen looked on. All independent political parties were suppressed or banned.[3]

Two of the more sinister names associated with the Third Reich began their political careers in Munich in this period. In March 1933 Heinrich Himmler became chief of all police forces in Bavaria. His chief assistant was Reinhard Heydrich. Soon, the Bavarian Political Police, which later became part of the Secret State Police (*Gestapo*), moved to its own headquarters in the Wittelsbach Palace on the *Briennerstraße* for more room. Their task was to eliminate all political opposition to the Nazi regime in Bavaria. By this time most of the jails were full of the regime's opponents. Therefore, two days after his appointment, on March 22, 1933, Himmler announced the opening of a new prison camp just outside of Munich at Dachau. Originally a munitions factory, Dachau became Germany's first concentration camp.[4]

Staffing the new concentration camps were the Brown Shirts, who considered themselves the true revolutionaries of the party. The SA led the book burnings that occurred throughout Germany on May 10, 1933. To purge the nation of their "un-German sentiments," party faithful in Munich culled books by Communists, Marxists, pacifists, and Jews from libraries, the university, and book stores, and burned them ceremoniously on the *Königsplatz*.[5] Yet despite the state-orchestrated violence, the book burnings, the suppression of political parties, the consolidation of political power, the harassment of Jews, Communists and Socialists, even despite the new concentration camps, the Brown Shirts still believed that the Hitler revolution had not gone far enough. The SA demanded that they be given more of the fruits of power, even command of a new "peoples' army." Throughout 1933 and into 1934 they marched through the streets of Munich rioting, breaking windows, bullying, demanding free beer in the beer halls, and extorting protection money from local businesses.[6] In short, they were becoming an embarrassment to the regime, which prided itself on having restored law and order to a chaotic Germany.

The Vice-Chancellor, finally realizing his and Hindenburg's mistake in appointing Hitler Chancellor, lamented the "permanent revolution from below." In a speech in June 1934 he suggested that perhaps it was time to restore the Hohenzollern monarchy in Berlin and bring an end to the Hitler government. Even more ominously however, the army was getting edgy: either the regime would solve the Brown Shirt problem, or the army would. Hitler had to act. On June 30, 1934, "The Night of the Long Knives," Hitler acted. Aided by Heinrich Himmler and Hitler's personal bodyguards, the black uniformed *Schutzstaffeln (SS)*, the regime arrested and shot the SA leader Ernst Röhm and almost 90 others in and outside the party whom Hitler deemed his enemies or "counter-revolutionaries." Among the dead was Kurt von Schleicher, a chancellor who had preceded Hitler and thwarted his rise to power, and Gustav von Kahr, the Bavarian leader who had double-crossed Hitler the night of the Beer Hall Putsch in 1923.[7] In August 1934 Hindenburg died and Hitler combined the office of President and Chancellor into the Office of the Leader (*Führer*). That same month, the armed forces swore allegiance and absolute obedience to Hitler personally, not the constitution. The seizure of power was complete.

Müncheners appeared to make very good Nazis. Overt resistance to the regime, at least in its early years, seemed non-existent. The distinguished historian of modern Germany, Gordon Craig, a student in Germany in 1935, recorded his observations of Munich years later:

> In those days in Munich, near the point where the Residenzstrasse empties into the Odeopnsplatz, there was a plaque on the side of the Feldherrnhalle to commemorate the death of the twelve Nazi 'martyrs' who had fallen there in November 1923, when Hitler's Beer Hall Putsch had been put down. On either side of this memorial stood an armed sentry, and pedestrians were expected, when they passed, to raise their arms in the so-called *Hitler Grüss*. They always did so, and I was surprised to discover, the first time I walked up the Residenzstrasse that, when busses went up the street, everybody aboard did the same— drivers, conductors, and passengers together, all of the arms sweeping up in dedicated unison, giving the impression that the vehicle was lifting itself off the pavement.

Craig describes Munich as a delightful city of "broad boulevards and leaping fountains" scarred by signs which read "Jews not wanted here."[8] But some *Müncheners* simply could not abide the regime. One such *Münchener* was "Pater" Rupert Mayer. Father Mayer was one of Munich's most popular priests and known in nationalist circles as one of Munich's most patriotic clergy. It was for that reason that nationalists and even right-wing politicians often invited Mayer to their events. Still, if the Nazis believed they could count on his support they were sorely mistaken.

Even before Hitler had come to power, Father Mayer had made it perfectly clear to his followers that he believed that a serious Roman Catholic could not simultaneously be a member of the NSDAP. The Nazis had signed a "Concordat" with the Vatican in 1933, which Hitler slowly yet continually violated. In addition, Mayer reviled the pagan and anti-Christian elements inherent in Nazism. The *Gestapo* put up with this opposition as long as they could, but finally arrested Mayer in 1937, stirring large protests throughout the city. Eventually released, the regime imposed a preaching ban on the cleric, which he ignored. Arrested again in 1939, the *Gestapo* sent Father Mayer to Sachsenhausen concentration camp. Released in 1940 because of ill health, Mayer spent the war years in internal exile in Ettal Cloister, two hours drive south of Munich, until spring 1945.[9]

Other clergy awoke too late to the threat that Nazism posed to Christianity in Germany. Many of them, including the Archbishop of Munich Cardinal Michael Faulhaber, had been won over early on by Hitler, especially after his speech of February1933 in which he claimed that "Christianity was the unshakable foundation of German civilization" and Bolshevism Germany's most dangerous enemy. When others, like Father Mayer, preached against the regime, Faulhaber urged caution. Only gradually, as it became clear that Hitler had no intention of safeguarding the rights of the church when those rights contradicted the interests of the regime, did Faulhaber's attitude toward Hitler change. One scholar has labeled Faulhaber's position as somewhere between "resistance and adaptability."[10] Unfortunately, this is where many *Müncheners* also found themselves.

To ensure "adaptability," the regime tried to establish a period of "normalcy" especially in Munich, which became a show place for the regime. The authorities went to great lengths not to tamper with the local beer hall. One observer has noted that the beer hall took the place of the church in the new regime as a kind of safety valve. The Bavarian slipped into the nearest beer hall, "instead of slipping quietly into the pew for prayer" to drown his sorrows listening to the deafening roars of the Bavarian brass band. "Without the beer halls, the German people could not endure the Hitler regime." But the beer hall really offered no refuge. In fact, the beer hall too served the regime's purposes. Nazi Party commissars visited the beer halls regularly, barking Nazi doctrines from the tops of the wooden drinking tables. Hitler's loyal followers received "spiritual guidance" listening to party commissars in the local beer hall.[11]

Drinking became a problem in the Third Reich. Political considerations aside, the regime had to watch the beer hall carefully. One scholar has estimated that in Hitler's Germany, alcohol consumption increased by 92%. In the early days of power, and in the war years, the regime had to remind its more ardent followers that "a National Socialist does not get drunk." Aside from the fights and destruction to property public drunkenness caused, health issues also caused the regime concern. In 1938 Heinrich Himmler argued in a speech that "no German has the right to impair his strength through alcohol abuse. Such action is detrimental not only to himself, but to his family, and above all, to his people." In fact, in Hitler's Germany habitual and "hereditary alcoholism" could be punished by sterilization.[12]

On coming to power in 1933, Hitler designated Munich the "capital city of German art" and ordered the city to highlight art that the regime deemed healthy for the "folk" such as landscapes, classical scenes, and depictions of a healthy and militaristic race. Hitler commissioned a new building, "The House of German Art" to display the regime's favorite artists. Completed in 1937, today it is simply known as the "House of Art" on the *Prinzregentenstraße* at the entrance of the English Gardens. In his speech opening the building, Hitler declared that if Berlin was the capital of the Reich, if Hamburg and Bremen the capital cities of Germany's nautical industry, and if Leipzig and Chemnitz the capital cities of German industry, "then Munich must once again become the capital city of German art." The regime tried to enforce that feeling of normalcy by sponsoring a "Day of German Art" in Munich every year. In 1939, the "day" lasted an entire weekend and turned all Munich into a showplace for Nazi art and propaganda. Art that the *Führer* designated as "degenerate" was now stripped from German museums including works by Kandinski, Monet, Klee, Beckman, Nolde and others.[13]

In 1935, Hitler also declared Munich the "Capital of the Movement" the most important city in Nazism. Local Nazi leaders installed plaques at all the "sacred" sites in Munich, including the *Hofbräuhaus, Feldherrnhalle,* and the *Burgerbräukeller.* As the birthplace of Nazism and the "Capital of the Movement," Munich hosted theatrical observances of Hitler's birthday, the date of his army enlistment, the battle of the *Hofbräuhaus*[14] and other anniversaries deemed important by party leaders.

Even though he was now ensconced in Berlin, Hitler often visited Munich. The National Party headquarters remained in Munich even though political power was concentrated in Berlin. The Party occupied the former Barlow Palace on the *Briennerstraße* and various Party offices lined the nearby *Karlstrasse.* Hitler had new offices built on the *Königsplatz* and surrounded these with shrines: the bodies of those killed in the 1923 *putsch* were interred in two "Honor Temples" on the east end of the square.[15] Hitler's mountain retreat and summer home at Berchtesgaden, where he went to get away from the tedium of government (and where he could meet his secret mistress, Eva Braun), lay two hours by car from Munich. When actually in

Munich, however, Hitler was not to be found in the beer halls any longer, unless he was giving a political speech. Usually, if he wanted to relax, Hitler would visit the "Osteria Bavaria" an Italian restaurant on the *Schellingstrasse* in Schwabing popular with the artist crowd. Hitler maintained a strict vegetarian life style and refused to drink alcohol, smoke tobacco, or eat red meat. According to Hitler's favorite architect and later Minister of Armaments, Albert Speer, at the Osteria Hitler would always look over the menu for several minutes, but inevitably ended up ordering mineral water and the ravioli.[16]

Hitler came to Munich every February 24th to celebrate the proclamation of the 25 Point Program in the *Hofbräuhaus* in 1920. But Hitler, ever the teetotaler, drank only mineral water. Because he was afraid of being poisoned, the manager of the *Hofbräuhaus,* Hans Bacherl, had to go to the basement accompanied by a fully armed SS guard and personally choose the *Fachinger* mineral water Hitler was to drink. In the *Hofbräuhaus* guest book, there was a special page reserved for the signature of the *Führer.* Once the war began, Hitler rarely attended these events.[17]

The 1936 Olympic Games were held in Germany. While the summer games were held in Berlin, the winter games were held in Garmisch-Partenkirchen, about a two hours drive from Munich. Because of its world renown, the Munich *Hofbräuhaus* was the location of the gala "Beer Evening" for visiting Olympic officials which was hosted by the Reich's Minister for Sport, Hans von Tschammer und Osten.[18] In the thirties, Munich became a playground for all the big Nazis, and the *Hofbräuhaus* usually figured in their games. One of Hitler's closest comrades was plagued with scandal in the 1930s, forcing Hitler himself to intervene. Hermann Esser, the Secretary of State and Tourism, a branch of the propaganda ministry, spent a little too much time in the *Hofbräuhaus.* Known for his many overt marital affairs, the forty year old Esser seduced the eighteen year old daughter of Hans Bacherl, the managing director of the *Hofbräuhaus.* After the birth of a child, Munich tongues were wagging. Mr. Bacherl confronted Esser on one occasion and it came to blows. Finally, Hitler had to step in and settle the matter. In 1939 he ordered Esser's wife to grant him a divorce, then he ordered Esser to marry Annie Bacherl. Hitler was the guest of honor at the private wedding that took place on April 5, 1939.[19]

By 1937 the *Hofbräuhaus* could claim that it was the largest beer producer in the world. On the first day of the "Reich Nutrition Exhibition" the *Hofbräuhaus* produced 49,500 liters of beer alone, the largest amount ever produced up to that time. Also, by 1939 the *Hofbräuhaus* had its own anthem. Ironically, a Prussian from Berlin, Wiga Gabriel, penned the words to a little waltz he called *"In München Steht ein Hofbräuhaus"* in 1936:

> In München steht ein Hofbräuhaus,
> ein, zwei, g'suffa,

da läuft so manches Fäßchen aus,
ein, zwei, g'suffa
Da hat schon manche brave Mann
ein, zwei, g'suffa
gezeigt was er so vertragen kann,
schon früh am Morgen fing er an
und spät am Abend kommt er heraus!
so schön ist's im Hofbräuhaus!

The song, played by German bands the world over ever since, is a constant refrain at any German Oktoberfest.[20]

The song became even more popular as the rich and famous flocked to Munich in the 1930s. The Duke and Duchess of Windsor and Charles Lindbergh repeatedly visited Munich in the 1930s. Lindbergh had a love interest in Munich. After the war, the famous pilot started a second, secret family with a Munich woman, while carrying on a third relationship with her sister. In 1937 John F. Kennedy, the future United States President visited Munich and the *Hofbräuhaus*. He and a friend spent several hours drinking there, and they befriended an SS man who encouraged them to take one of the clay HB mugs as a souvenir, even going so far as tell the Americans which door of the beer hall to sneak out of undetected. As they did so, they were immediately apprehended by a waiter who confiscated the mug and threw out the two miscreants. Looking back Kennedy saw the SS man roaring with laughter. Kennedy visited Munich three more times before World War II, and always made the *Hofbräuhaus* one of his stops.[21]

The most famous American visitor to Munich in the 1930s had to be the author Thomas Wolfe. In his book, *The Web and the Rock,* he declared that Munich was a "German paradise." "How can one speak of Munich but to say it is a kind of German heaven?" "The best beer in Germany, in the World, is made there and there are enormous beer cellars that are renowned throughout the land." The main character in the novel, visiting the city, loved "the roaring tumult of the Hofbrau Haus" [sic] where he "felt the warmth, the surge, the powerful communion" of the locals as they "gulped down from stone mugs liter after liter of the cold and powerful dark beer." Wolfe also describes his first visit to the Oktoberfest. At first he was disappointed: too many people, too loud and rowdy, and Germans all around. It all appeared to him as a "less brilliant Coney Island." After the first few beers, and after the band played the obligatory "Ein Prosit" at which the entire beer tent rose to sing together, the *gemütlichkeit* finally possessed him. "And now there was no strangeness any more. There were no barriers any more. We drank and talked and ate together. I drained liter after liter of the cold heady beer."[22]

Tourists could ignore the less appealing side of Nazism. Natives could not ignore the approaching storm. The clouds could already be seen, especially in Munich. In September 1938 the infamous "Munich Conference" took place in the *Führer's* private headquarters on the *Königsplatz*. Hitler demanded the *Sudetenland* in Czechoslovakia and was ready and willing to go to war to get it. This area adjoining the German border with Czechoslovakia, with a mixed German and Czech population, had never been German. No one except Hitler wanted war in 1938. In fact, had Hitler pressed for war and actually sent German troops into Czechoslovakia, some army officers, led by Colonel-General Ludwig Beck, stood ready to kill the leader. Instead, Benito Mussolini proposed a peace conference, held at Munich. After much haggling, Mussolini for Italy, Chamberlain for Great Britain, and Daladier for France, agreed to force the Czechs to surrender the *Sudetenland* to Germany. The military opposition to Hitler crumbled, and elated *Müncheners* celebrated the *Führer's* statesmanship in the streets. By appeasing Hitler, Chamberlain, Daladier, and Mussolini believed they had avoided war. And they had avoided war. In March 1939 Hitler simply took the rest of Czechoslovakia.[23]

Even as the beer was flowing in endless liters, life was becoming more and more difficult for the regime's enemies, and especially Jews. The Nazi regime directed actions against the Jews of Germany almost as soon as they came to power in 1933. A boycott of Jewish shops and businesses in April 1933 was less than successful from the regime's point of view. In April 1933 the "Law for the Restoration of the Professional Civil Service" and later the "Law for the Protection of German Blood and Honor" removed Jews from almost all aspects of German professional life. In 1935, at a special session of the *Reichstag* held at Nuremberg to correspond with the "Reich's Party Rally" held in that city every year, the regime passed the Nuremberg Racial Laws. The laws forbade most professional, social, and economic contact between Germans and Jews. The government forcibly deported all non-German Jews. The regime hoped that all these measures would lead Jews to leave Germany. By May 1938, 3,500 Jews had already left Munich and Bavaria. This still did not satisfy the regime, who wanted a Jew-free Germany as quickly as possible. If Jews would not leave voluntarily, maybe they could be forced to emigrate.

In November, the Nazi regime found their excuse to unleash terror against Germany's Jews. In Paris, a Jew (Herschel Grynspan) shot a German diplomat (Ernst von Rath) to protest Germany's forced deportation of Jews. In response, the Nazi leadership, which happened to be in Munich for the commemoration of the 1923 putsch, called for a violent reaction. The Munich leadership called for rallies in all the large meeting places and beer halls in the city to confront the problems of "world Jewry." At a meeting in Munich's Old Town Hall, on November 9th, Hitler's propaganda minister, Dr. Josef Goebbels, called for pogroms against the Jews of Germany. He ordered all Jewish shops, homes, and businesses destroyed and synagogues burned. Thugs set fire to the Jewish Synagogues on *Herzog-Rudolf-Straße* and *Reichenbachstraße* and Jews throughout the city were dragged from their homes, beaten in the streets, then marched off to concentration camps. The event became known as *"Kristallnacht"* ("Crystal Night") for the reflection of the broken glass and windows of Jewish shops lying in the gutters the next day. On 10 November city authorities in Munich demanded that keys to all Jewish owned businesses be turned over to the government. Munich authorities refused to allow the destroyed Jewish enterprises to reopen.[24]

Once war erupted in Europe on September 1, 1939 the Jewish position deteriorated even further. At first, the Nazis demanded that Jews live in special ghettos, isolated from the general population. In March 1941 the Munich regime established a Jewish ghetto and relocation center at Milbertshofen, a northern suburb of Munich. But by 1942 the regime in Berlin had changed policy once again. In January 1942, the regime had decided upon the "Final Solution of the Jewish Question." Jewish ghettos and "relocation centers" were to be emptied and the inhabitants shipped Eastward, to Poland, for "Special Handling" which meant extermination. In 1942 Milbertshofen was closed and the inhabitants shipped Eastward to almost certain death. Only eighty-four of Munich's Jews survived the Nazi dictatorship.[25]

The methods for killing had been worked out even before the war. In 1939 the regime sanctioned what came to be known as the "T4 Euthanasia Program." Through this program, the regime hoped to exterminate the mentally ill and the incurably insane whom the regime termed "life unworthy of life" (*Lebensunwertes Lebens*). The victims were evacuated from hospitals into specially designed vans or rooms into which carbon-dioxide gas was fed until they died. The bodies were then cremated. Hitler himself reportedly approved the use of carbon-dioxide as the best means for the killing. The policy continued into the war years until 1941 when Germany's churches, especially the Roman Catholic Archbishop of Muenster, Clemens von Galen, publicly protested the measures and the regime.[26]

Thus, as the war progressed, the true nature of the dictatorship, if it was not already apparent, became abundantly clear. Still life went on as normal for many. The old rituals were still observed. Hitler appeared at the beer halls of Munich yearly to commemorate the Party's triumphs. On November 8, 1940 Hitler appeared at the *Löwenbräukeller* to commemorate the Putsch. (He could no longer give the annual speech at the *Bürgerbräukeller* which had been damaged in an assassination attempt on the *Führer* in 1939). A year later, on November 8, 1941 he declared in his speech that never before "has a giant empire been smashed and struck down in a shorter time than Soviet Russia." He spoke too soon. A year later, at the same location on November 8, 1942 Hitler learned that the Western allies had landed in North Africa and taken German military planners by surprise. The hand writing was on the wall for the "Thousand Year Reich." Hitler appeared one last time at the *Löwen-bräukeller*, on November 8, 1943 but that was his last appearance in Munich's beer halls to commemorate the *putsch*.[27] By summer 1944 American and British bombers were flying over Germany at will. By summer 1944 it was clear that the war was lost. The only way *Münchener's* could escape the increasingly inevitable defeat, was to try and kill the man who had brought them to it.

7. *From World War to* Weltstadt, *1939–1958*

Adolf Hitler once promised that if Germans entrusted him with the leadership of the country they would not be disappointed. "Give me four years, and you won't recognize Germany again." It took him a little more than twelve years, but the *Führer* fulfilled his promise. By spring 1945 all of Germany lay in ruins. Though the war, which broke out in 1939, had gone well for Germany in the first few years, by 1944 the handwriting was clearly on the wall for the "Thousand Year Reich." The Allies had firebombed Hamburg in 1943 and by early summer 1944 American and British bombers reached Munich. Repelled on all fronts by Americans and British in the West, and Russians in the East, some Germans took matters into their own hands.

There had been attempts to kill Hitler even before the war. Some of the assassination attempts occurred in Munich. In 1938 a Swiss, Maurice Bavaud, tried to kill Hitler in Munich by shooting him. Bavaud might have shot and killed Hitler had not bystanders in the crowd intervened and knocked the pistol from his hands. The *Gestapo* arrested and later executed Bavaud. The most famous attempt on Hitler's life to take place in Munich occurred a year later, at the *Bürgerbräukeller* on November 8, 1939. The bomb plot was the work of one man: Georg Elser. Elser knew that Hitler came to Munich every year and gave a speech at the famous *Bürgerbräukeller* beer hall to commemorate the *putsch* of November 8–9, 1923. In the months leading up to the event in 1939, Elser, a carpenter, visited the beer hall regularly. Clandestinely, he carved out sections of the pillar near the podium Hitler would use and planted a time delayed bomb to go off during Hitler's speech. However, on the fateful night Hitler ended his speech several minutes earlier than usual in order to catch a train. When the bomb went off, it killed several people still inside and destroyed the beer hall. The *Führer* escaped unscathed. Elser was later caught at the border with his carpentry tools trying to get to Switzerland.[1]

The true nature of the dictatorship only became clear to many Germans during the war years. Many people did not like the revelation. Aside from the war, the killings, and the concentration camps, the regime's actions began to effect the average Germans in ways they did not like. Protesting the regime and overt resistance, was difficult but not impossible. For example, in April 1941 the regime unleashed a campaign against the Roman Catholic Church. Hitler, and many of his followers, had always held that Christianity was a religion for weaklings. Bothered by overt expressions of faith, in 1941 the regime began removing crucifixes from Bavarian schools and public buildings. The public outcry was so great that Hitler personally rescinded the order in August 1941. Hitler reportedly exploded that if Bavarian Gauleiter Wagner tried to do anything so "stupid" again, he would personally send him to Dachau.[2]

In Munich, the most famous resistance group was the "White Rose." The "*Weiße Rose*" consisted of several students at Munich University, inspired by Hans and Sophie Scholl, Christoph Probst, Alexander Schmorell, Willi Graf, and at least one sympathetic faculty member, Professor Kurt Huber. Their "resistance" consisted of painting anti-Nazi graffiti on the walls of the university main building, and spreading anti-Nazi leaflets denouncing the regime as "evil" and "inhuman." Some of the students had served on the Russian front and knew about some of the atrocities taking place, and that the war could not be won. At the Battle of Stalingrad, which had ended disastrously for the Germans in February 1943, the Germans lost 250,000 men and the Russians captured over 90,000 officers. The Russians even captured the commander of the main army group, Field Marshall Friedrich von Paulus, and thereby eliminated the German Sixth Army. The *Weiße Rose* insisted that good Germans should not hope for "the military victory over Bolshevism, but the defeat of National Socialism." They paid for their resistance with their lives. On 18 February 1943, the students secretly distributed their flyers at the university while classes were still in session, hoping to remain undetected. Nevertheless, they were discovered by the janitor, arrested, and immediately turned over to the Gestapo.[3]

As Germany's defeat in the war became more evident, the attempts on Hitler's life became more desperate. The most famous assassination attempt on Hitler was the Army Bomb Plot of July 20, 1944. A large group of conspirators including generals, politicians, civil servants, even clergymen, plotted to get rid of the *Führer* by killing him with a bomb in his headquarters in Poland. They hoped to negotiate an end to hostilities, and thereby save Germany from total annihilation (despite the fact that at the Casablanca Conference of 1942, Great Britain, the United States, and the Soviet Union had agreed to accept only an unconditional surrender). Claus Schenk Graf von Stauffenberg, a highly decorated military officer, agreed to deliver the bomb concealed in a briefcase, and place it near Hitler during a military conference. During the conference, however, someone moved the briefcase. When the bomb exploded it killed several people in the room, but only grazed Hitler.[4]

Nevertheless from that point onward, officers were not permitted to carry their side arms anywhere near Hitler. The *Führer* no longer gave public speeches. In fact, Adolf Hitler's last public speech was in the *Festsaal* of the *Hofbräuhaus* only a few months before, on 24 February 1944. The speech marked the anniversary of the "Twenty-Five Points" of the National Socialist Party, announced at the same location in 1920. Only the "Old Comrades" had been invited to attend, and Hitler refused Dr. Goebbel's repeated requests to have the speech broadcast over the radio. Reportedly trembling and gaunt, he told the "old comrades" that he believed now more than ever in the final victory and that the imminent Allied (D-Day) invasion in the West would fail. Germany would obtain its revenge on the West and the Jews who, in his mind, had started the war in the first place.[5]

A year later many of the same "old comrades" met again in the *Hofbräuhaus* to once again commemorate the "Twenty-Five Points," but by now the military situation was far worse. The bombs started falling on Munich in April 1944 so that by 24 February 1945 the *Hofbräuhaus* was already substantially damaged. Hitler had no desire to view such damage, nor could his safety in the city be guaranteed: American and British bombers roamed the skies over Munich at will. Therefore he sent a telegram to his followers gathered in the cold damp beer hall to remember the party's twenty-fifth birthday. In Berlin, Hitler celebrated the event with a little ceremony of invited *Gauleiter* from Munich. Hitler was physically unable to stand for long periods of time so that the commemorative proclamation had to be read out by Hermann Esser. "Twenty-five years ago I prophesied the victory of our movement. Today I prophesy the victory of the German Reich."[6]

But the Reich was crumbling all around them. On June 6, 1944 Great Britain and the United States had finally opened up a western front against the Germans in France, and by August Paris had been liberated. By spring 1945 the Americans and British had crossed the Rhine River and were heading for the heart of the Reich. The Russians, too, were closing in on the Reich from the east. Most major buildings in Munich had received some form of damage; many were completely destroyed. The towers of the *Frauendom*, Munich's medieval cathedral, were still standing, but the nave and most of the chancel had been destroyed. Most of the churches in the city had been destroyed, as were all the major beer halls. As for the *Hofbräuhaus*, by April 1945 the upper floors and the *Festsaal* had been completely destroyed and by war's end only the ground floor of the *Schwemme* remained usable. In

December 1944 bombers had destroyed the *Löwenbräukeller* on the *Stiglmaierplatz* and reduced most of the building to soot and ashes. The *Bürgerbräukeller* on the *Rosenheimerplatz* was "unrecognizable" and looked more like an "unused trolley barn" than a beer hall. Most of the food, including all of its beer, wine and cheese, had already been looted by the natives when the Americans arrived in April. Ironically, Hitler's private apartment on the east side of town remained undamaged and would later be used as offices for the American army.[7]

On April 28, an organization known as the Bavarian Freedom Movement (*Freiheitsaktion Bayern*) tried to take over the city to prevent "senseless resistance" and further destruction. Commandeering tanks and weapons, one regiment attacked to the northwest toward Augsburg in an effort to break a way through to the American lines in that town. The *Freiheitsaktion* cooperated with rebel soldiers and attacked guards around the Dachau concentration camp where the stronger prisoners in good enough health joined the liberation movement. Fighting inside Munich drove the Nazis to the East end of town, when the Freedom Movement appealed directly to the local population for help. Via radio they encouraged the citizens of Munich to "descend into the streets and spread this news to everyone you met [sic] . . . Workers! Leave your factories. We appeal especially to *Wehrmacht* officers and soldiers to discontinue this senseless slaughter of the enemies of the Reich and join us in bringing it to an early end." That morning General Ritter von Epp proclaimed himself "provisional leader of the Bavarian Freedom Movement" and "Governor General of Bavaria." In a radio broadcast he declared that, "in the name of humanity, as well as common sense" Germans should "throw off the yoke of Nazism" so that the killing would cease. By 4:00 P.M. armed SS troops were moving into the city to put an end to the von Epp "putsch."[8]

Two days later, on April 30, 1945 American troops reached the center of Munich, about an hour after Hitler and his new wife had killed themselves in Berlin. When the American Third Infantry Division finally reached the city to link up with the Forty-Second Rainbow division, there was no one in the city to offer a surrender. "A strange feature of the capture of this most Nazi German city was the warm reception the United States troops received. Women threw flowers . . . Residents came running out of houses to smile and wave at the soldiers even before the shooting died down. It was the gayest welcome for United States troops since France," the previous summer. "No officials were left to surrender Munich. They had left with troops who had escaped southeastward two days ago."[9]

The first US soldier to reach the center of town that afternoon related a surreal experience. Liberated POWs, old men, women, and children all turned out to greet the Americans at the *Mariensäule* in the center of town in front of the *Rathaus* with the famous *Glockenspiel* clock. A few paces later, past more ruins, the troops came upon the wreckage of the *Hofbräuhaus.* Only a part of the *Schwemme* (ground floor) remained intact. The rest of the beer hall, and most of the buildings on the *Platzl,* lay in ruins. Almost the whole city was destroyed. It would be a long time before the taps would flow again and the mugs filled with golden, frothy beer. Still the American troops inspecting the ruins of the famous beer hall took away as souvenirs anything marked with the famous "HB" symbol.[10] Munich now belonged to the victors. For the people of Munich, now was the time for clearing the rubble, rationing of food, and fake beer. The Germans refer to this period as the "*Stunde Null,*" the "Zero Hour."

The city appeared as a scene from a Hitchcock movie. Most of the fires had burned out by the time the Americans arrived. According to a *New York Times* reporter on the scene "the spires of the great cathedral loomed in the crystal-clear air against the towering Alps' peaks in the background. Munich did not look like a city under attack. It did not look like a city at war."[11] Still photographs of the city show the center of the old town, including the cathedral, in ruins. Military Government came to Germany with "White Lists" containing the names and prewar addresses of people they believed could help in the postwar administration of Germany. On May 1, a Military Government detachment arrived and called the former Lord Mayor of Munich before 1933, Dr. Karl Scharnagl, out of retirement to run the city again.[12] "The Bavarian National Museum is still intact- though empty and the Rathaus is still usable and there the military government unit, under the command of Major Eugene Kelly [sic] Jr., . . . has been set up."[13]

At the time, no one knew what was to be done with Germany or Bavaria or Munich for that matter. The infamous "Morgenthau Plan" still circulated in American circles. "The men and women in the German labor force can best serve themselves and the world by cultivating the German soil" Morgenthau had written. Under his plan, France would get the Saarland and Rhineland; Poland would get East Prussia and Upper Silesia, the Ruhr would be internationalized and all German heavy industry would be destroyed. "Germany's road to peace," Morgenthau stated, "leads to the farm!" What was left of the country after that was to be divided into two states, North and South; members of the Gestapo and SS were to be used as slave labor in rebuilding and reconstruction.[14]

And that reconstruction was not going to be easy. By most eyewitness accounts, Munich was a disaster. After more than 70 air attacks, 81,500 homes were completely destroyed (out of 262, 000 homes in 1939) and most others were severely or partially damaged. Sixty percent of the pre-war population (480,000 people) still lived in the city.[15] British experts, brought in to survey the damage, thought it would take at least "fifty years" to rebuild the city. The British even suggested that the citizens forget about rebuilding the city and simply move to another spot on the Isar River.[16]

As a result of bombings and combat, 6,632 *Müncheners* had been killed, another 15,000 wounded, and approximately 20,000 residents of the city had died on the various combat fronts throughout the war. The city's native population had shrunk from about 824,000 people in 1939 to approximately 470,000 by war's end.[17] Former concentration camp inmates, slave laborers, displaced persons, and former prisoners of war now flocked to the city in search of food, medical attention, and whatever shelter they could find. This actually led to overcrowding in the city which now had to be administered and fed by the United States Army. Food was so scarce throughout Europe in the first years after the war, especially in Germany and eastern Europe, that hunger was common. Even in Great Britain, bread was rationed for the first time in the nation's history. In the Western zones of Germany, the normal daily ration was to be 1,550 calories but rarely reached this level. Some got more if their profession warranted, some got less. Manual laborers and farmers received more while an unemployed civilian was supposed to survive on between 1000 and 1500 calories daily.[18] The black market thrived.

In June 1945 the occupation authorities banned the brewing of beer to conserve grain and took over most of the major beer halls and breweries in the city. The Bavarian authorities tried to convince the military authorities that beer was not a luxury item but a major staple of the Bavarian diet which provided much nutrition, but they had little success. "*Dunnbier*" and "*Hefesud*" a poor, non-alcoholic substitute, made their debut, at least until the military authorities got the breweries running again and the food situation stabilized.[19] Ironically, perhaps, American troops, often accompanied by attractive Munich women, drank so much beer in their off hours, in some cases paying with American dollars, that they inadvertently resurrected the Munich food and beer industry in spite of military government prohibitions. They also clearly ignored the "non-fraternization" orders by finding German girlfriends so quickly. The *Bürgerbräukeller*, for example, now became a popular American canteen.[20]

The Declaration of Berlin was issued on June 5, 1945 which stated that even though Germany remained a single political entity, sovereignty would be temporarily exercised by the occupying powers. The zones established for the convenience of the Allied powers were not supposed to represent permanent annexations or a political division of Germany. The German armed forces, not the civilian government, signed the surrender agreements. This was symbolic: it demonstrated that the Allies would not recognize any German political (i.e., Nazi) authorities. Of course, by spring 1945 there were no political authorities. The top Nazi leadership were either dead, had fled the country, or were in Allied custody.[21] Military authorities outlawed all forms of entertainment and postal circulation and they enforced a strict curfew. Bavarians were not permitted to use the telephone. Travel by any means other than bicycle or foot was prohibited. All shops except those selling food remained closed and all motor travel by civilians was limited to physicians, nurses or clergymen traveling to outlying parishes.[22]

Joint Chiefs of Staff Directive 1067 strongly reflected American intentions of occupying Germany not as a liberated country, but as a "defeated enemy nation." The directive made no distinction between "good Germans," those who might have opposed the Hitler dictatorship, and the "bad Germans" that supported the regime. According to the directive, there was only one Germany, and it was National Socialist and militarist.[23] The directive ordered the removal from office of all leading officials of the National Socialist regime and party, members of the police forces, especially the secret and security police. JCS 1067 ordered the removal and arrest of members of the SS, all members of the General Staff, leaders of the SA, and top officials in all ministries of state. Also, JCS 1067 ordered the removal of officers above the rank of lieutenant in the civilian police and all judges and lawyers who had served the Hitler regime.[24]

The directive ordered the removal of those who held office or "were active" at any level from local to national in the party or its organizations; those who took part in atrocities or racial persecutions; "avowed believers" in National Socialism or its racial or militaristic creeds, and those who gave support or political assistance to the party or its leaders. The directive prohibited these persons from employment and positions beyond "ordinary labor" for any reason.[25] Military authorities had the right to review and even veto decisions of German courts and authorities that contradicted Allied occupation statutes.[26]

Soon, however, these strict restrictions began to soften. Although the Allies forbad "fraternization" between military personnel and Germans, that restriction broke down almost immediately. There were approximately 1.6 million American military personnel stationed in Germany by May 1945, and, once the shooting stopped, they began looking for companionship. Many soldiers found German girlfriends shortly after hostilities ceased.[27]

American military authorities quickly realized that they needed local German talent to get the country moving again. Dr. Scharnagl had already been appointed Lord Mayor of Munich. On May 28, military authorities appointed Dr. Fritz Schaeffer Minister-President of Bavaria. He quickly assembled a team of leaders to start running the state again. Though he had never been a Nazi, many of the people he felt he needed in his administration were former Nazi party members. This directly contradicted Allied and American policy, which stated that anyone with a Nazi past be forbidden from employment. However, the commander of US forces in the occupation zone agreed with Schaeffer. General George S. Patton Jr., employed former Nazis to get the trains and communication lines running again, and to help in the daunting task of reconstruction. There was simply no one else available. As criticism of his practice of hiring ex-Nazis continued to grow, Patton brushed aside the criticism of Schaeffer, reportedly saying that "Nazis are just like Republicans and Democrats." In September, General Eisenhower and Military Government removed both Schaeffer and Patton from their posts.[28]

Military Government then appointed Dr. Wilhelm Hoegner Minister-President of Bavaria. Hoegner, a Social Democrat, had served for years as a delegate in the Bavarian Parliament and the national *Reichstag* in Berlin. During the war, he served as a contact between American Intelligence Services and Social Democrats living in Germany. Hoegner vowed to hire only those people that had never been National Socialists, and to comply with American occupation policy. The day of his appointment, September 28, 1945 the United States officially reconstituted the State of Bavaria which Hitler had abolished in 1934.[29]

Nevertheless, it was already clear to American and German authorities that JCS 1067 was not working. Therefore, on March 5, 1946 Military Government and German authorities worked out what became *"The Law for the Liberation from National Socialism and Militarism."* The "Liberation Law" required every adult German to fill out and submit a questionnaire (*Fragebogen*) detailing their record in the Third Reich. The law established five categories of Germans: Major Offenders; Offenders (activists, militarists and "profiteers"); Lesser Offenders (those to be placed on probation); Followers, and Persons Exonerated.[30] All Germans were classified into one of the categories based on their *Fragebogen*. The Minister-President of the state had to appoint a "Minister for Political Liberation" to oversee enforcement of the law. The Minister for Political Liberation "must be an opponent of long standing of National Socialist tyranny and militarism, actively pro-democratic, and an avowed supporter of the principles of this law."[31]

The Liberation Law set up a system of tribunals *(Spruchkämmern)* for processing the questionnaires. Each tribunal had one chairman and at least two assessors, all 30 years of age or older. The chairman could only be a qualified judge. A public prosecutor served at each tribunal. The tribunals decided the classification of persons according to their questionnaires and imposed penalties. Appellate tribunals existed for the review of decisions.[32] There were 316 de-nazification tribunals and eight appellate courts operating in the U.S. Zone.[33]

The first *Spruchkammer* trial in Munich began on June 15, 1946. In the dock was the janitor from Munich University, Jakob Schmitt. Schmitt was the janitor at the University of Munich who apprehended Hans and Sophie Scholl of the White Rose in February 1943 and turned them over to the

Gestapo. The tribunal classified Schmitt, a "Major Offender" and sentenced him to five years at hard labor. Another famous de-nazification hearing took place on October 27, 1946. This time the famous folk-singer from the *Hofbräuhaus*, Weiß Ferdl, was in the dock. He had apparently celebrated the advent of the regime in 1933 in many of his skits and songs. "One no longer has to listen to Saxophones, no longer must we dance the Rumba or the Charleston. Away with jazz and the nigger dance, we're no longer *meschugge!* Now we can hear what we like, marches and German music pleasing to the ear." But Ferdl only joined the party in 1940 so the tribunal classified Ferdl as a "follower" and fined him RM 2000.[34]

The *Hofbräuhaus* received a new manager in 1945 as well: Valentine Emmert replaced Hans Bacherl, who, as we have seen, had been very close to the regime. Emmert started to patch up the beer hall as best he could so that within a year the first *Fasching*, Bavaria's Mardi-Gras celebrations, could be held in the *schwemme*. Even by fall 1946 there was limited food available and meat was scarce. Food was still rationed, and then only purchased with coupons: the *Reichmark* was now worthless. Beer remained watered down. Military Government officials allowed a small "Fall Festival" to be held in 1946 and there was some beef but only fake beer. Only in 1949 would the first real "Oktoberfest" be held again, and then with only three beer tents.[35]

In Munich, the economic situation had reached crisis proportions by 1948. The Potsdam Agreements of June 1945 ordered some twelve million ethnic Germans out of Poland and eastern Europe and their relocation in Germany. Many of these ended up in western Germany along with those that had fled the Russian advance in 1945. Though relocation camps had been built throughout Bavaria, there simply were not enough to house all of the displaced persons. Dachau became home to many of these displaced persons when the Allied authorities transformed the former camp into a displaced persons center. Protests and riots erupted in the camp in 1948 as wood, food, and fuel became scarce. Cramped conditions, lack of bedding, even lack of straw led to a week long hunger strike in September 1948.[36] Western Allied Authorities had to do something, and quickly.

The occupation authorities realized that Germany could not remain prostrate much longer. Relations between the western Allies and Russia had broken down, so that obtaining a unilateral peace treaty with Germany had become impossible. And the costs of the occupation and administration of Germany continued to rise. In 1948 the United States announced the Marshall Plan which promised economic assistance to any country rebuilding from World War II. Germany readily accepted the money and simultaneously carried out a currency reform, replacing the old *Reichmarks* with new *Deutschmarks*. Economic recovery seemed to happen overnight. The black market disappeared, food became more available, and the raw materials for making proper beer began to become available. To encourage economic growth and cut their costs, Great Britain, France and the United States merged their zones of occupation into one single economic unit in 1948 united by the new currency. This would later become West Germany.[37]

Throughout 1948 and into 1949 delegates from the states in the western occupation zones met to write up a governing document for a West German state. Presented on May 23, 1949, the Basic Law (*Grundgesetz*) became the legal basis for the Federal Republic of Germany. The delegates pointed out, however, that they did not consider the document a constitution. Rather, they intended the Basic Law to be merely a governing document until the "whole of Germany" (i.e, the Communist east) could freely vote on a new document. The Lord Mayor of Cologne, Konrad Adenauer had presided over these deliberations and, through his influence, the capital city for the new German state became Bonn, the birthplace of Ludwig van Beethoven and Adenauer's home town.[38]

A new Germany emerged in 1949, but leftover issues from the old Germany kept arising, especially in Munich. In 1948 the famous folk singer Karl Valentine died, and a year later Weiß Ferdl followed him to the grave, symbolizing the true end of the folk singing culture in Munich. In 1949 Munich's most famous musician, Richard Strauss died. Strauss had been born in Munich in 1864 and his mother, Josephine was a daughter of the famous Pschorr brewing family. Strauss was a musical child prodigy and his fame spread throughout Europe before the Nazis came to power. After 1933, the Nazi government very much wanted to tote Strauss as its model musician. In 1933 Strauss was elected president of the "*Reichsmusikkammer.*" But Strauss insisted on working with a Jewish librettist, Stefan Zweig, with whom he wrote "The Silent Woman" or *Schweigsame Frau*. In addition, Strauss had a Jewish daughter-in-law and, therefore, partly Jewish grandchildren. Thus, by 1935 he had fallen out of favor with the Nazi regime and resigned the *Reichsmusikkammer.* One scholar has argued that Strauss was not a Nazi, nor was he an anti-Nazi. "He was one of those who let it happen." Still, because he held office in the Nazi regime, Strauss had to appear before the Munich de-nazification tribunal. On June 8, 1948 the tribunal cleared Strauss of any guilt. Strauss died in Garmisch on 8 September 1949. The same tribunal classified Karl Fiehler, the Nazi Mayor of Munich an "Active Nazi." The tribunal confiscated twenty percent of his wealth and forbade him from any profession for twelve years. He ultimately served five years in prison.[39]

In 1949 an American couple donated the material needed to rebuild Munich's famous *Glockenspiel* clock in the Town Hall. They hoped that by doing so "all races and nationalities and religions could enjoy the pleasure of the *Glockenspiel* together . . ." In the same year the mayor of Munich, Thomas Wimmer, instituted a program for "cleaning women" to help remove the rubble from the city. Sometimes known as the *"Wimmer-Dammerl"* ("Wimmer's Girls") they were popularly known as the *"Trümmerfrauen"* ("The Rubble Ladies"). The campaign to remove the rubble and rebuild the city as fast as possible came to be known as the *"Rama dama"* campaign for *"Räumen tun wir"* ("We're Cleaning Up!"). The workers shoveled the rubble onto trains which carried the refuse to the outskirts of town. Bakers and butchers provided the workers with snacks and food, Munich's breweries supplied free (fake) beer.[40] Still, it was only in 1950 that real full beer was served again for the first time since the end of the war.[41]

Then tragedy struck. Fasching, or Mardi-Gras was celebrated in Germany beginning on January 6. This day marked the end of the Christmas season and the beginning of the season of balls and parties leading to Ash Wednesday and the penitential season Lent. The *Hofbräuhaus* marked the beginning of the celebrations with a Viennese Night of Waltzes in the famous festival room on January 7. Late that evening, a fire broke out which severely damaged the roof and barrel-vaulted ceilings. This seriously set back reconstruction of the institution. It took an hour to bring the fire under control as the Mayor of Munich and Finance Minister looked on in horror.[42] City planners had agreed to rebuild Munich, at least the old city quarter, as closely as possible to the way it appeared before the war. Since the *Hofbräuhaus* was a vital landmark and tourist attraction, the beer hall too would be rebuilt as traditionally as possible.[43]

In terms of beer commerce, 1951 marked a special year. The Hunting and Costume Parade, the traditional parade held on the opening day of Oktoberfest was the largest ever held up to that time. The parade, which opened the Oktoberfest on September 23, 1951 included two-hundred and forty Folk Groups, forty-eight brass bands, forty festival beer wagons, and 8000 participants that marched through the city. The Oktoberfest itself was the largest ever. The *Löwenbräu* tent alone sold fifty-five thousand liters of beer on the last weekend of the festival, demonstrating that at least Munich's beer industry had recovered.[44]

But there were growing pains. In the 1950s, both tourists and locals alike began to complain about the service in the world's most famous beer hall. Patrons, among them some powerful Bavarian politicians, accused the manager of the *Hofbräuhaus,* Franz-Xaver Trimborn, of ordering the waitresses to pull the mugs away from the barrel before they were completely full to the liter mark. Some visitors complained that the food served was substandard but the prices high. An ambitious Bavarian politician, Franz Michel, summoned Trimborn before the economics committee of the Bavarian Parliament to answer charges that he was cheating loyal *Müncheners* out of their beer and serving bad food. In fact several members of the committee complained that they, too had been less than satisfied with the beer and food in the *Hofbräuhaus,* causing an uproar in the committee. Through what one observer has described as a combination of Bavarian charm and righteous indignation, Trimborn was able to successfully refute the charges. To the food charges he replied that when anyone complained to him about bad food he refunded their money. As to the beer charge he replied that he would "gladly pay five thousand marks to the man who could invent the machine that would measure out a serving of beer to the exact liter." Then, he suggested sardonically, maybe all the complainers would "shut up and have some fun." Even though an "Association Against Short Measures" had been established in 1899 to inspect beer service in the city, the Nazis banned the organization. Only computers could solve the problem of under-filling the mug. Computers and modern technology have solved Trimborn's dilemma. Today, when a liter mug is placed under the tap the machine measures out exactly one liter of beer in just six seconds. Still, if the computer fails to measure out a proper *maß* of beer, or if there is too much foam, the good Bavarian sends it back to be refilled. Reconstituted in the 1980s, The "Association Against Short Measures" meets the first and third Tuesdays of every month in the *Hofbräuhaus.*[45]

Part of Herr Trimborn's troubles was a rumor going around Munich that the *Hofbräuhaus* used preservatives in the beer. Some *Müncheners* even filed a law suit, demanding to know what precisely was in the beer. Since the *Hofbräuhaus* was owned by the Bavarian State, the litigants believed they had a right to know everything that went on in the beer hall. The finance minister himself got out in front of the controversy and stated that *Hofbräuhaus* beer was brewed strictly according to the 1516 beer purity tradition. This was important, since the *Hofbräuhaus* was such an important cultural (not to mention economic) asset, measures had to be taken to ensure that the institution remained genuinely Bavarian. Still, Trimborn was able to "modernize" the beer garden by adding tables and chairs. Patrons of the beer garden no longer had to stand around empty beer barrels, but could sit in the garden and enjoy their favorite drink.[46] Despite the first pessimistic assessments, fires and delays, it took less than fifty years to rebuild the city, or the *Hofbräuhaus.* In fact, under Trimborn by 1958, the *Hofbräuhaus* had been entirely rebuilt. The entire establishment could seat three-thousand, five hundred people. The great *"Festsaal"* on the third floor finally reopened just in time for the 800th anniversary of the city. Also, Munich celebrated the birth of its one millionth citizen, making it a truly metropolitan city.[47]

It took Munich 13 years to undo some, though not all, of the damage Hitler and the war had wrought on the city. By 1958 the city had achieved a level of normalcy, and Munich had become Germany's most popular city. Tourists from all over the world once again flocked to the city and the *Hofbräuhaus* in the 1950s. In 1950, the famous African-American dancer,

Josephine Baker, visited the city and performed in the Congress Room of the German Museum. Baker had a mixed history with the city. In the years after the Hitler Putsch of 1923, the city government had prohibited a Baker performance as too lascivious for Munich and better suited for Berlin. Baker traditionally danced in "a banana skirt and little else" and the city fathers thought that was too risque for Munich. "No, mademoiselle, you will not dance in Munich, a city that respects itself" they responded to her request for a permit. In the postwar years however, Ms. Baker visited Munich and the *Hofbräuhaus* regularly, visiting the famous beer hall whenever she visited the city.[48]

By the 1950s Wiga Gabriel's *"Hofbräuhaus Song"* was already popular in Germany and around the world. Louis Armstrong visited the city in the 1950s and played *"In München steht ein Hofbräuhaus"* on what the press described as his "golden trumpet." American troops felt so at home in Munich that the 9th Infantry Division formed their own *"Trachtenkapella"* a brass band complete with their own *Lederhosen*. They traveled throughout Germany giving concerts of mixed American and Bavarian favorites, including the *Hofbräuhaus* song. Others to visit the *Hofbräuhaus* in this period included Mario Lanza, Gina Lollabrigitta, Bridget Bardot and W. Somerset Maugham, who usually ordered a radish, sausages and beer.[49] By 1958 Munich was able to make the claim that it was a truly cosmopolitan city, a *"Weltstadt"* famous the world over for beer and fun as well as art and culture. After 1958, the *Hofbräuhaus* could claim that it was "the most famous beer hall in the world."

8. *The Most Famous Beer Hall, the Most Popular City*

On June 14, 1958 Munich awoke to the sound of trumpets blasted from every tower and rooftop in the city. The trumpets heralded the eight-hundredth birthday of the city, founded in 1158. At precisely eight-thirty in the morning, every church bell in the city sounded: Munich was eight-hundred years old. This was a rude awakening, for the night before some 500,000 *Müncheners* and guests had watched a torchlight parade through the center of the city with over two thousand floats. The floats depicted historical figures from Munich's past. Parade organizers removed from the parade a float of Lola Montez, the Spanish dancer that cost Ludwig I his throne after a request of the Wittelsbach family. The partying went into the small hours at all of the major pubs and beer halls. Celebrations continued throughout the day and in the evening a gala performance of Mozart's "Marriage of Figaro" was performed in the newly restored Cuvillies Theater.[1] Munich had almost recovered from World War II.

The year 1958 had become a finish line of sorts. The citizens of Munich worked hard to ensure that most of the city, especially the old historic part of town, was rebuilt in time for the 800-year celebrations. In fact, the theme of the anniversary festivities proclaimed that "Munich is Munich Again."[2] The city to which those million inhabitants awoke on that cool June morning was surrounded by parks, meadows and hills that had not existed before the war. Before the city could rebuild *Müncheners* had to clear the rubble from the streets. The city built a railway through the town so that people could dump refuse and rubble on to it as the train passed by their homes and streets. The rubble was then taken to the edge of town and dumped where it was then covered by topsoil, planted with grass and trees and transformed into the series of parks and hills which surround the city. Munich has since grown beyond these artificial boundaries, and much of that growth occurred in the 1950s and 1960s.

Still, even as late as 1958 the city was not totally rebuilt. Forty-five percent of the city had been destroyed in World War II, and by 1958 reconstruction was only sixty percent completed. Despite more then ten years of reconstruction projects, Mayor Thomas Wimmer complained that the city was still 50,000 apartments short. Munich needed much more office space, classrooms, hospitals, and affordable housing. Refugees from eastern European (Soviet) territories had transformed the city into a microcosm of European society as a whole.[3]

Reconstruction became fraught with political tension even into the fifties and sixties. "Traditionalists" demanded that the city be rebuilt as close as possible to what it had been before 1939. "Modernizers" demanded that the old, bombed out buildings be replaced with modern structures to permanently mark the destruction Hitler had brought to the city and the nation. The two sides came to a compromise by the 800th Anniversary celebrations: the Old City was rebuilt as close as possible to resemble the Munich before 1945. Outside the old city walls, as the city expanded outward, buildings would be rebuilt traditionally if possible, but modern where necessary. By the 800th anniversary of the city, many of these buildings, including the *Hofbräuhaus*, had been rebuilt so carefully, that people could not tell where the destruction had occurred.[4]

Munich had become West Germany's most dynamic city with all the attendant problems of a metropolis: monumental traffic problems, expensive shops that offered a variety of fine merchandise, first rate schools, and a prestigious university, hardly any unemployment, and a generous social welfare system. Munich had the largest university in West Germany, Ludwigs-Maximilians University. Munich possessed the first atomic reactor, a world class academy of music, and one of the most vibrant artist colonies in the world. Already by 1958 Munich could claim to be the intellectual and cultural capital of all Germany. It was also fast becoming the technology capital of Germany. Several major scientific and technology companies that had been located in the Eastern areas of Germany or Berlin before 1945, moved to Bavaria and Munich after the war. Osram and Siemens Electrical companies, and Messerschmitt-Bölkow-Blohm aeronautics concern all located or relocated their headquarters to Munich after the war, making the city a major location for the electrical industry and aerospace technology. These new companies needed many more educated workers so that, in the 1960s and 1970s, several new universities were established such as Regensburg, Bayreuth, Passau and Bamberg.[5]

Munich once again became the beer capital of the world. In 1958 there were 1,643 breweries, and the larger Munich breweries pumped out thousands of gallons of beer every day.[6] Munich now became the number one tourist destination in Germany and the *Hofbräuhaus* the number one tourist site in the city. Often, if an American got into a Munich taxi and requested to be taken to Schwabing or some other destination, the cab driver would ignore them and take them to the *Hofbräuhaus* anyway, figuring that they were confused. Still, after visiting the *Hofbräuhaus* a few times, tourists also made their way to the other entertainment spots in the city, including Schwabing, the bohemian artistic district just north of the university. In addition to many fine restaurants, Schwabing was home to several jazz clubs, then later "twist" clubs and bars.[7] American influence in the city became easily recognizable. Aside from the hundreds of tourists that came to the city every year, American troops were stationed in Munich and in Augsburg, and they became a boon to the local economy. Jazz music, Coca-Cola, blue jeans, and in the 1960s and 1970s, *Mc Donald's, Burger King,* and *Kentucky Fried Chicken,* became staples of the Bavarian fast food diet.[8] The local beer hall, however, refused to conform. The *Hofbräuhaus* served only traditional Bavarian meals, and served only the house beer. In postwar decades, the beer hall became a Bavarian oasis in an increasingly multi-cultural city.

And the *Hofbräuhaus* was not alone. In 1958 the *"Mathäser Bierstadt"* beer hall on the *Bayerstraße* near the central train station underwent a substantial renovation. In an attempt to offer direct competition to the *Hofbräuhaus,* the *Mathäser* billed itself as "the largest beer hall in the world" with over 7000 seats.[9] Dark and somewhat dreary on the inside, the *"Mathäser* Beer City" never had the tradition or the *gemütlichkeit* of the *Hofbräuhaus.* The *Mathäser* served *Löwenbräu* beer and was more popular with locals than tourists. When tourists came to Munich, they went to the *Hofbräuhaus* which came to be synonymous with the city.

One observer noted in 1961 that Munich was "the liveliest city in Germany and . . . the most rounded in view of its music, its flourishing theater, its concentration of culture." Munich was already a favorite tourist destination for Americans, who "like the atmosphere in Munich restaurants, where strangers are expected to take vacant seats at occupied tables, Bavarians are friendly and like to talk."[10] The swarm of tourists that visited the city greatly taxed the facilities of the *Hofbräuhaus,* the reconstruction of which had been completed by 1958. But by the middle sixties increased demand required another renovation and expansion. The management enlarged the kitchens and installed a new stove, "the largest in the world" at the time, to keep up with demand. On August 1, 1963 the *Schwemme* reopened after a four month renovation designed to make the hall brighter and cleaner. Lighter, golden hued frescos replaced the darker traditional paintings on the ceilings. By October 1965 the management had completely renovated the beer gar-

den and surrounding buildings and added terraces and patios to accommodate expanded outdoor dining facilities.[11]

Munich witnessed the opening of the 1960s with the transfer of power
from the immediate postwar generation, to a younger one. On March 27,
1960 Hans-Jochen Vogel became Mayor of Munich. Vogel, a young, thirty
four year old lawyer marked the shift in political leadership and represented a
new youthful era in Munich politics. With over one million people in the city,
Vogel's immediate problem was to build more affordable housing. Moreover,
with the population ever increasing, sanitation and public transportation
would all have to be improved.[12]

Then the first student protests erupted. In Munich, the first "student
revolt" actually occurred in 1962, six years before the 1968 student protests
that rocked the continent. One historian has noted that things always happened in Munich first, before they happened elsewhere in Germany. On June
20, 1962 a melee ensued when residents of Schwabing called the police on a
street musician for disturbing the peace. When police arrived, students came
to the defense of the musician. When police called in reinforcements, more
students arrived. Battles between the "youth" and the police followed. There
were several injuries and several arrests. Mayor Vogel and the Police Com-
missioner, Schreiber concluded that "psychological factors" were involved:
the students were really protesting "authority" and "wealth." A staff psy-
chologist was added to the police department to handle such conflicts in the
future. Other police departments throughout Germany followed what came
to be called "the Munich Line" and began using psychology to understand
group dynamics to better train police. Later in the decade, there would be
two deaths in Munich when student revolts ripped through Germany in
1968.[13] These conflicts often spilled over into the beer hall. In the *Hofbräuhaus* there were often fights between the locals and American soldiers
that some times required intervention.[14] Politics is always a lively discussion in
the *Hofbräuhaus,* and in the era of the Vietnam War, political disputes often
occurred between Americans and Germans in Munich's beer halls.

Military topics have always been contentious issues in Germany since
World War II. Ten years after the defeat of Hitler's Reich, the North Atlantic
Treaty Organization asked West Germany to form an army for its defense.
The Paris Agreements of 1954 requested that Germany raise an army of
500,000 men and officers. Most Germans, however, dreaded war and
protested the decision to create the *Bundeswehr,* the Federal Defense Force.
In Augsburg that year, angry youth pelted the defense minister with beer
steins. Several incidents in Munich give us a sense of the antipathy of Germans to their new army. For example, in October 1956, a brawl broke out on
a Munich bus. When a teenager was asked to move to allow an elderly person
to sit, he motioned to some soldiers on the bus insisting that they should

move, not him. When fighting ensued, and the bus could not complete its rounds, the police had to be called. That same month, twenty teenagers attacked two uniformed soldiers in a Munich street, severely beating them and stripping them of their insignia. At the Oktoberfest that year, angry civilians harassed five *Bundeswehr* soldiers relentlessly, driving them from the festival. *Münchener's* did not want another German army.[15]

Federal authorities went to great lengths to make sure that the *Bundeswehr* shared little of the qualities of Hitler's *Wehrmacht*. A member of parliament, Theodor Blank, received the duty of establishing the new defense force. Blank, and General Wolf Count Baudissen insisted that the new force not be a "collection of robots . . . with weapons." Blank and Baudissen attempted to copy the ideas of the reform generals Scharnhorst, Boyen, and Gneisenau who, in the days of Napoleon's occupation, transformed the defeated Prussian army into a revitalized citizen's militia. They sought to establish an army of "citizen soldiers under arms," soldiers infused with a strong democratic spirit.[16] Blank, under strict parliamentary supervision, built the *Bundeswehr* into a military force fully integrated into the North Atlantic Treaty Organization. Yet the effectiveness of this fighting force, at least in its early years, seemed doubtful.

In the fall of 1962 the armies of N.A.T.O. participated in exercises known as the "Fallex 62 Manouevre." In the exercises, *the Bundeswehr* performed miserably. Germany's most popular news magazine, *Der Spiegel,* and many people in the Defense Ministry, felt that this was a direct result of the policies of the Federal Defense Minister: the Bavarian Franz Josef Strauss. On October 10, 1962 *Der Spiegel* published an article entitled "Conditionally Ready for Defense." N.A.T.O awarded the "conditionally ready for defense" label to the West German army after the Fallex 62 exercise, the lowest grade on the N.A.T.O. scale. The exercises presumed that an invasion from the east would begin the Third World War. The results of the exercises made up the body of the article. According to N.A.T.O., had there actually been an attack, most of Northern Germany would have been occupied within only a few days; between 10–15 million civilians in Western Europe would have been killed outright by ground and air attacks, and chaos would have been "indescribable." The article asserted that communications would be demolished and facilities for the care and medical treatment of retreating civilians would have been "completely inadequate." Above all, the article said that Germany's nine divisions remained ill-equipped, undermanned, and short of officers, and that there would have been no weapons for the German reservists.[17]

A few weeks later, in the middle of the night, on October 26, 1962 the Security Division of the West German Federal Criminal Office raided the offices of *Der Spiegel.* That same weekend, also in the middle of the night, the police arrested the publisher of the magazine, Rudolf Augstein, and the author of the article, Konrad Ahlers. In fact, the police actions lasted the entire weekend, 26 through 28 October 1962. The raids and arrests had been ordered by the Defense Minister, on the grounds that the article had violated national security, and that the authors had divulged state military secrets.

Many suspected more personal reasons behind the police actions. After the Chancellor, Konrad Adenauer, the *Spiegel's* next favorite political target was the defense minister, the Bavarian Franz Josef Strauss. *Der Spiegel* held the boisterous Bavarian in very low regard. Born in Munich on September 6, 1915 Strauss had been one of the founding fathers of the Christian Social Union, the Bavarian sister party to the Christian Democratic Union, the conservative party of the popular Chancellor of West Germany since 1949, Konrad Adenauer. Strauss, like Adenauer, tended to be autocratic and secretive, and very conservative. He demanded almost absolute obedience from the army even during peacetime. Though this technically accorded with the *Basic Law*, the *Spiegel* felt that Strauss took the idea to the limit and dangerously beyond the spirit of the constitution. Also, the *Spiegel* found Strauss' ideas on the role of the military in a democracy problematic. On the contrary, Strauss reintroduced many of the elaborate ceremonies and traditions of the old Imperial German army into the new defense force, traditions which many found to be contrary to the spirit of a "democratic" army. Lastly, the *Spiegel* opposed Strauss' ideas concerning defense, especially his belief in a preventive first-strike against Eastern forces in any conflict, and his insistence on a nuclear, as opposed to a conventionally oriented defense.[18]

As a result of the arrests, a storm of protests swept through Germany. The *Bundestag*, the Federal Parliament, began its own investigation into what came to be called the "*Spiegel* Affair." Before the *Bundestag*, Strauss admitted that he had not only ordered the arrests, but that he had also ordered the German military attache in Spain to request the extradition of Ahlers (who had been on vacation) after first denying it. The questions quickly began to take on the theme, "What did the Chancellor know, and when did he know it?" The Adenauer government began to crumble. As Chancellor Adenauer made preparations to cut his losses and fire the Defense Minister to save his coalition, Strauss began to speak more openly before the *Bundestag* about the government's participation in the affair. He claimed, for example, that he had personally informed the Chancellor of the proceedings against the *Spiegel* on the 18th, 22nd and 23rd of October, well in advance of the raids. This Adenauer fervently denied.[19]

More ominously, during the searches and the arrests of Augstein and Ahlers, the Federal Minister of Justice, Wolfgang Stammberger, had not even been awakened or informed. Stammberger only became aware of the raids the following morning, Saturday 27 October, by reading the newspapers. He had not even been notified that the Adenauer administration was considering such actions. He soon realized that the oversight was intentional.[20] Because of this insult, the Free Democratic Party, Stammberger's party, pulled out of the governing coalition with the Christian Democratic Union/Christian Social Union. After negotiations, the parties agreed that, for the F.D.P. to return and save the Adenauer government, Strauss would have to be fired as Defense Minister, and Adenauer would have to promise to retire sometime in the near future. Adenauer agreed to retire in 1963, and dismissed Strauss.[21]

Strauss returned briefly to government, serving as finance minister in the "Grand Coalition" government of CDU/CSU and SPD in 1966–1969. But then he returned to Bavaria where he became Minister-President and, according to one observer, ruled the former kingdom in "regal style." Branding himself a "Progressive Conservative," Strauss opened up Bavarian industry to East Germany and the Soviet Union. During Strauss' tenure, Bavaria became one of the richest states in the Federal Republic, and Munich became the most popular city in Germany. Right into the 1980s, however, Strauss' critics continued to complain of his authoritarian style and conservatism. Youth even held a rock concert in August 1979, "Rock against Strauss" to protest his "aggressive and reactionary politics." Nevertheless, Munich gave Strauss a hero's funeral after he died while hunting in the Bavarian forest in October 1988.[22]

Germans engaged their past in various forums. In the schools, universities, and special research institutions scattered throughout the city, some of the best appraisals of the Nazi years came from scholars working in Munich. In 1947 officials from the states in the American occupation zone proposed opening an "office for political documentation" to store all the documents being generated by the Nuremberg War Crimes Trials. The office would maintain an archive, sponsor research in its holdings, and publish a scholarly journal. Delegates, meeting in the fall 1947, agreed that the office would be an independent (i.e., not affiliated with a university) research institute dedicated to the study of the history and crimes of the Third Reich. The delegates agreed to house the institute, known as the *Institute for Contemporary History* today (*Institut für Zeitgeschichte*), in Munich. It is the premiere research institute for Third Reich studies in Germany.[23] In music, plays, even the lively cabaret scene all reviewed Germany's rise from the ashes of the Hitler dictatorship. One visitor to a Munich cabaret made fun of all the jokes he heard about the Hitler years while in Munich. "You laugh a lot about Hitler here" this observer remarked to a Bavarian acquaintance. "We always did" the Bavarian replied, " that was the trouble."[24]

One of the other problems confronting the *Hofbräuhaus* that still confronts the institution today is the theft of the mugs with the world famous "HB" symbol embossed on them. While once in a while a mug was stolen as a souvenir (and during the military occupation, hundreds of mugs were taken by American G.I.s) by the 1960s and 1970s the problem had reached crisis proportions. In 1966 two patrons were caught smuggling out twenty-five steins. Female customers even dressed as if they were pregnant in order to smuggle the mugs out of the building. It is estimated that in the decade 1960 - 1970, 250,000 steins disappeared from the *Hofbräuhaus*. In the decade 1970 - 1980 tourists removed 300,000 steins as souvenirs. (In 1972, when the Olympic Games were held in Munich, 500 steins a day disappeared from the *Hofbräuhaus*). When the tourists and souvenir seekers began to rummage through the private cupboards and steal the mugs of the regular customers, something had to be done. Therefore, in the 1970s the management installed a system of "stein lockers" in the *schwemme*. At first there was room for two-hundred one-liter beer mugs. Later a second bank of lockers made room for another two-hundred mugs so that today there is room for at least 424 steins. So great is the demand for a private stein locker that even one hundred more would not satisfy demand. A locker becomes free only when the owner dies, moves away, or otherwise terminates membership. Sometimes lockers are even handed down within families.[25] Several beer halls, including the famous *Andechs* Cloister Brewery not far from Munich, have special lockers for the mugs of their regular customers. This has stopped the theft of membership mugs, and severely limited the amount of mugs stolen generally.

Hans-Jochen Vogel's most ambitious plan while mayor was to convince the International Olympic Committee to hold the 1972 summer games in Munich. Preparing for the Olympics would provide the impetus to correct Munich's many infrastructure problems. The city had simply become too large too fast. New housing communities would have to be built, more roads, and mass transit would have to be completely revamped in order to accommodate the games and the city's continued growth after the games had ended. The tourist dollars generated from the games would more than reimburse the city for its investment.[26] When it was all over, the *Hofbräuhaus* would find itself in the middle of a metropolis.

Campaigning for the games began as early as 1965. The city council believed that hosting the Olympics would crown the city's international image. The event would also help remove the stigma of Munich as the "capital city of the movement" of the Nazi years. In fact, Munich had been trying very hard to repair the fault between it and its former Jewish citizens. Many had fled Germany after the war vowing never to return. Still, in the 1960s Munich invited its former Jewish citizens from all over the world to visit Munich for up to fourteen days. All expenses would be paid by the city. Three people visited in 1961, and that number rose to forty-seven by 1965.[27]

The city convinced Olympic officials that they could provide the infra-structure and support needed to host the games, and that the games would bring in lots of tourist dollars to help with the ongoing expansion of the city. In April 1966, Munich won the competition to hold the 20th Olympic Games in 1972. The city began construction on a new Olympic Stadium and associated Olympic Village with apartments, student dormitories and community, cultural and sport facilities. In a novelty for the period, the village would even have an underground parking garage. Even *Playboy* magazine featured "The Girls of Munich" in its August 1972 edition, in anticipation of the Munich Olympiad.[28]

It would be the biggest Olympic Games ever. And even though it cost roughly $600 million to prepare the city for the games, Munich citizens paid just twelve cents on the dollar to host the event. The city raised most of the money by selling commemorative Ten Mark coins, lottery tickets, and selling television and radio rights to broadcast the games. The German army agreed to "donate" 22,000 reservists to augment clean up and maintenance crews.[29] As the city expanded to make way for the Olympic Games, the *Hofbräuhaus* had to expand as well to accommodate the ever increasing numbers of tourists. In the 1970s the *Trinkstube* was enlarged by expanding into and renovating neighboring buildings in anticipation of the hordes of visitors to the city.

But the Olympic games failed to blot the image of Munich's connection with the Third Reich. Tragedy struck the games when Arab terrorists took the Israeli Olympic team hostage. Even though the Palestinian terror-group "Black September" had carried out several terror attacks in the Middle East, Western Governments failed to take the group seriously until September 5, 1972 when they struck again on the unsuspecting Israeli athletes. In the early morning hours the group stealthily infiltrated the Olympic Village, stormed the Israeli apartments, and seized most of the Israeli athletes, refusing to release them until and unless Israel released Palestinian prisoners it was holding. They also demanded that the German Government release two members of the notorious Baader-Meinhof terrorist organization. The Israelis refused, and German negotiations with the terrorists broke down. The terrorists then demanded a plane to take them and the hostages to Egypt. An attempt by German police forces to free the hostages at the airport in *Fürstenfeldbruck,* rather than let them be transported to Egypt and almost certain execution, ended in gunfire. The debacle resulted in fifteen dead, including all of the hostages. The event dashed the hopes of many who believed that the games would finally mark a new era in the history of the city and the nation. Instead, a city which sought to obtain an international reputation as a tourist destination and commerce center, was suddenly transformed into a stage for an international conflict that continues to this day.[30]

Violence and sports seemed common in Munich in the 1970s. During the European Cup Finals games in 1979 where Nottingham England played Malmö Sweden, tempers flared to such a degree between fans of the teams that for the first time, beer was served in paper cups in the *Hofbräuhaus*. The management feared that the fans would destroy the place with the heavy stone and glass mugs in which the beer was usually served.[31] Political violence too, seemed to be part of life in Europe and Germany throughout the 1970s. In this decade, domestic terrorism, at least in Germany, came from the radical political left. Two pseudo-Marxist groups, The "Baader-Meinhof" group and the "Red Army Faction" kidnaped and killed industrialists and politicians. The RAF even hijacked a Lufthansa German airlines flight in 1977. They forced the plane to land in Africa and demanded the release, from German prisons, of their compatriots. German Rapid Deployment forces stormed the plane and freed the passengers.[32]

In the 1980s however, Right-wing political movements became more active. These nationalist organizations had come and gone in Bavaria, as they did throughout Europe in the postwar period. The *"Deutsche Volksunion"* or *"German Peoples' Union"* had its headquarters in Bavaria in the 1950s and 1960s. Then in the 1980s came *"Die Republikaner"* or *"Republicans"* led by a former journalist and SS man name Franz Schönhuber. Generally these parties possessed an anti-foreigner program, and championed an outdated form of extreme German nationalism. They aimed at being alternative political parties, not terrorist organizations. But right-wing terrorists arose as well. In September 1980, "Neo-Nazis" set off a bomb at the Oktoberfest to protest the increase of foreigners into the city. Thirteen people were killed and 219 injured. Sporadic Neo-Nazi violence and threats have continued to plague Munich, Germany, and other European nations such as France and Great Britain to the present day.[33]

Nevertheless, throughout the 1980s the tourists continued to come by the thousands. Even the rich and famous continued to visit the world's most famous beer hall. No trip to Munich was complete without such a visit. George Bush (as vice President of the USA), the Apollo 15 crew members, and countless others made their way to the *Platzl*. In 1987 the directors of Munich's six major breweries voluntarily drafted and signed a "Renewal of the Beer Purity Law" on St. Andrew's Day, November 30, 1987. To commemorate the 500th anniversary of the original Beer Purity Law, the breweries pledged to use nothing but hops, barley, and pure water. This way, Bavarians would know that the beer they drank was pure, as more and more imports appeared on the Bavarian market.[34]

The steep rise in demand for Bavarian beer necessitated a newer, larger brewery by the 1980s. The *Hofbräuhaus* had simply outgrown the brewery complex on the Innerer-Wiener Straße. Fortunately, around the same time, the city had outgrown the little airport at Riem, the former race track and air-field on the outskirts of town. The city decided to build an entirely new, modern airport near Erding, a forty-five minute train ride from the center of the city. *Hofbräuhaus* bought the former airport site upon which to build a much larger and more modern brewery. The new facilities would permit *Hofbräuhaus* beer to become a major player on the international beer market as well.[35] As early as 1980 plans were underway to move the brewery apparatus from the *Hofbräukeller* location, to the larger space on the edge of town. There, the *Hofbräuhaus* brewery would have almost limitless space to expand its operation as demand continued to grow. On November 23, 1988, the new brewery, which took eight years to complete, opened just in time for the 400th anniversary of the *Hofbräuhaus am Platzl*.[36]

9. *400 Years of* Gemütlichkeit

September 27, 1989 marked the 400th anniversary of the *Hofbräuhaus am Platzl* and *Hofbräuhaus* beer. Beginning in June 1989, and continuing throughout the year, the *Hofbräuhaus am Platzl* celebrated its 400th anniversary. *Zweites Deutsches Fernsehen*, German TVs channel 2, filmed a special documentary on the event and issued a souvenir VCR tape of the official celebration, with a commemorative CD, a relatively new medium for the time. The *Hofbräuhaus* issued a special collector's edition 400th anniversary *Hofbräuhaus* stein as well. In addition, *Hofbräuhaus* issued a commemorative book (*400. Jahre Hofbräuhaus Festschrift*) discussing the history of the *Hofbräuhaus am Platzl* and the new brewery. The celebrations demonstrated that the *Hofbräuhaus* was a vital institution of the city and the Bavarian state, intricately tied to the history of the city and its economy.[1]

In the 1980s Michael and Gerda Sperger became the managers of the *Hofbräuhaus* and they set out to make sure that the *Hofbräuhaus* remained more than just a tourist attraction: they were determined to ensure that it remained a prime example of authentic Bavarian culture. The menu was revised and several more *stammtische* were added to accommodate the increase in *stammgäste*. Under the Spergers, the number of membership tables rose to over 100 and there are now over five thousand *stammgäste* members visiting the *Hofbräuhaus* on a regular basis. In fact, in the 1980s members constituted over half the regular visitors to the *schwemme*. Many of the regular members had first come to the beer hall with their fathers or grandfathers.[2] It was to this tradition, preserved for four hundred years, that Bavarians reaffirmed in 1989.

All the major Bavarian politicians got in on the act, congratulating the institution on its 400th birthday. Dr. Max Streibl, Minister-President of Bavaria, wrote that the Bavarian might not be the best gourmet, but he knows great beer, and Bavarians have recognized the quality of *Hofbräuhaus* beer for 400 years. Finance Minister Gerald Tandler, wrote that the *Hofbräuhaus* had been inextricably linked with the city of Munich. The *Hofbräuhaus*, he wrote, had become the image carrier of Bavarian culture to the world. Perhaps the most poignant testimonial came from Georg Kronawitter, the Lord Mayor of Munich. He remarked that Munich's "unofficial anthem" linked the *Hofbräuhaus* forever with the city. The "unofficial anthem" to which he referred is "Solang der Alte Peter:"

> Solang der Alte Peter, der Petersturm noch steht,
> solang der grünen Isar durch d' Münchener Stadt noch geht,
> solang da drunt am Platzl noch steht das Hofbräuhaus,
> solang stirbt die *gemüatlichkeit* in München niemals aus!

> [As long as the tower of St. Peter's Church still stands,
> as long as the green Isar River continues to run through Munich,
> as long as people can have fun on the *Platzl* and the *Hofbräuhaus* still stands,
> the *gemutlichkeit* will never die in Munich!].

And not only in Munich: so many tourists had visited the city, that Mayor Kronawitter acknowledged that the spirit of friendship and merriment ("*Gemütlichkeit*") associated with the *Hofbräuhaus* had been transplanted throughout the world.[3]

More momentous events in Berlin soon overshadowed the 400th anniversary celebrations. There, on the night of November 9, 1989, East German authorities opened the Berlin Wall, the visible symbol of the forced division of Germany that had divided the city since 1961. Revolution had been brewing in eastern Europe ever since Mikhail Gorbachev, premiere of the Soviet Union since 1985, announced his policies of political openness (*Glasnost*) and economic restructuring (*Perestroika*). Seeing the freedom and openness of Soviet society, the peoples of eastern Europe began to press their own governments for "openness" and "restructuring." This led to the collapse of the Soviet instituted regimes in Poland and Hungary by 1988. By autumn 1989 it was clear that the Soviet Union would not send in troops to save corrupt communist regimes, as it had done repeatedly since the end of World War II.

The fact that the Soviet Union would not intervene in the internal affairs of its allies encouraged the East German people to demand political openness and economic reforms in their country. Throughout 1989, hundreds of thousands of East Germans protested the Stalinist regime of Erich Honecker, the security chief turned premiere who had supervised the construction of the Berlin Wall in 1961. When Honecker cracked down on the protests, East Germans began to take "vacations" in Hungary, from where they could then simply drive or walk across the border to Austria, and from there get to West Germany. When the Honecker regime refused to issue travel visas to Hungary, the protests in East German cities became even more heated. The Soviet

Premiere, Gorbachev, visited East Germany in October 1989 for the fortieth anniversary of the East German state. By then, hundreds of thousands of East Germans had either fled or were held up in West German embassies in Poland, Hungary, and Czechoslovakia demanding passage to the west. Those that remained used the Gorbachev visit to mount massive protests against their own leadership and in favor of Gorbachev's reforms movement. Demanding "We are the People" hundreds of thousands protested in all the major cities of East Germany, but especially Leipzig every Monday night, demanding political freedom. Gorbachev warned Honecker that he would not use Soviet forces to maintain him in power. Gorbachev urged him to consider seriously the demands of the protestors. "History punishes those who delay" he is reported to have told the East German leader.[4]

However, the larger the protests grew, and the louder the demands for reform became, the harder Honecker cracked down. As soon as Gorbachev had returned to Moscow, on October 9, Honecker ordered that soldiers use live ammunition to put down demonstrations in Leipzig and Berlin. The result would have been slaughter, and maybe even civil war, had not one of Leipzig's most famous citizens, Kurt Masur, not intervened. Masur, the director of East Germany's most prestigious *Gewandhaus Orchestra*, met that evening with Honecker's security chief, Egon Krenz, and persuaded him to countermand Honecker's orders. After all, Masur knew many of the protestors personally, since thousands of dissidents met regularly every Sunday in the orchestra's headquarters in Leipzig. Deserted by his own men, the Honecker dictatorship collapsed, crushed by the will of the people. The Politburo then removed him from power on October 17th and replaced him with Egon Krenz, who promised immediate reforms.[5]

But Krenz could not deliver reform fast enough. With Honecker gone and the fear of terror removed, the authority of the regime collapsed. Throughout October and early November, hundreds of thousands continued to protest and demand reforms, while thousands more simply fled the country every week. What could the regime do? They hoped that by relaxing travel restrictions to the west, they could stem the tide of refugees out of the country. Therefore, on November 9, 1989 East German authorities announced that, as of that evening, East Germans could travel to the west simply by showing their identification. That very evening East Germans began to test that policy. Thousands appeared at the various border crossings, especially those at the wall and demanded to cross. The overwhelmed border guards let them. The border guards did not have time to check with their superiors, who probably only wanted one or two border crossings opened. Instead, border guards opened all the gates on that cold November night. The swell of people was so great, that parts of the wall had to be removed to accommodate the travel. That was the end of East Germany. The process of reunification could begin, something the East German people began to demand almost immediately.[6]

That evening, and on into the weekend of November 10–12 1989, hundreds of thousands of East Germans crossed the border into Western Germany. Many went to see West Berlin for the first time in their life, while some traveled to other parts of Germany to visit friends and relatives they had not been allowed to see for twenty-eight years or more. Many came to Munich. The Bavarian authorities declared that the "Ossies," as they came to be called because they were from East (*Ost*) Germany, could use public transport, visit museums, and use health spas for free. The city permitted stores and shops to stay open on Sunday (something not allowed even to this day) so that merchants could cope with the demand from a massive wave of East German shoppers.[7]

And they came to the *Hofbräuhaus am Platzl*. According to one estimate, 6000 East Germans found their way to the *Hofbräuhaus* the first weekend after the wall's opening. The Langer family from Chemnitz held their family reunion there after a morning of shopping. There is a picture of them in the *Bild Zeitung* newspaper with friends and family they had not seen in years, sampling the *Hofbräuhaus* dark beer. Five Easterners sat at a table and ordered a beer, but when patrons realized they were from East Germany, they bought them round after round of beer. They drank free all night. "Harald, Ralf, Detlef and Ingeborg" from Brandenburg dreamed of "doing something crazy" and driving to Munich for years. They finally did it that weekend in November. They drove twenty-four hours across Germany just to visit the *Hofbräuhaus*. Making their way to the *Platzl*, they stayed for a few hours, took part in the general revelry, and then drove all the way home. One easterner lost DM 20 in an automat. The *Hofbräuhaus* waiters took a collection and sent the man home with DM 50.[8]

West Germany, Bavaria, and Munich paid East Germans "welcome money" when they arrived in the city. This policy originated in the 1950s to encourage defection from the East and to help refugees get settled to their new life in the West. However, with the huge number of East Germans now flooding Munich, the city authorities declared that it could only pay the welcome money until the end of the year. In December, Munich's mayor George Kronawitter issued an appeal to *Müncheners* to rent out any spare rooms and beds in anticipation of the "Christmas Rush" of East Germans expected to flood the city for the holidays. Chaos plagued the city in December when some 60,000 East Germans swarmed into the city. The *Theresienwiese*, where the annual Oktoberfest is held every year, had to be turned into public parking to cope with the amount of traffic in the city[9]. A small national reunion occurred in Munich's *Hofbräuhaus* that weekend and similar reunions occurred in every major city in Germany. This led to a growing movement for the reunification of the German people and the two German states. That reunification finally occurred less than a year later, on October 3, 1990.

The opening of Eastern Europe also meant the creation of new markets for *Hofbräuhaus* beer. In the nineties, demand for *Hofbräuhaus* beer increased so drastically that the brewery had to be expanded once again. As a result of this expansion, the *Hofbräuhaus* brewery became one of the largest breweries in the world, increasing output by 15.7%, over 250,000 hectoliters a year.[10] But of course the tourists came too, in the hundreds of thousands, increasing even more the demand for *Hofbräuhaus* beer.

Some of these tourists were famous. Mikhaill Gorbachev, one of the political leaders responsible for Germany's reunification, and his wife Raisa, visited Munich in March 1992. They ended what the Munich newspapers called a "triumphal visit" by visiting the famous *Hofbräuhaus*. The management closed the *schwemme* early on March 6, 1992 to prepare for the important and prestigious visit. Guards turned away most tourists at 3:30PM that afternoon. Gorbachev, the man most people in Europe credited with tearing down the Iron Curtain and allowing the reunification of the Germanies, arrived at 7:30 to an overflowing crowd in the *Festsaal*. Donning a Bavarian hat with a genuine "*gamsbart*" (goat beard) brush, the last leader of the Soviet Union joined the revelers in singing the famous *Hofbräuhaus* song.[11] Gorbachev was not the only famous visitor to the *Hofbräuhaus*. The American author Arthur Miller, the crew of the Apollo 15 Space Mission, Nelson Rockefeller, George Bush (while Vice-President) and Arnold Schwarzenegger all visited the *Hofbräuhaus*.

In 1975, the city of Munich designated most of the old city as a "pedestrian zone." The city forbid all motor traffic on the *Neuhauserstraße,* the street leading from the Karl's Gate to the *Marienplatz*. The city also closed the Sendlingerstraße to cars so that most of the old town city center became a pedestrian only zone. To celebrate the twenty-fifth anniversary of the "pedestrian zone" in 1997, the *Hofbräuhaus,* as well as all the other beer halls in the old city, offered guests a special menu with traditional Bavarian fare and discounted beer specials.[12]

That same year, the *Hofbräuhaus* celebrated another milestone in its history: 1997 marked the one-hundredth anniversary of the renovation of the former brewery into the most famous beer-restaurant in the world. Officially, the celebrations were set for November but the partying actually began in August and rose to a crescendo in November. Plans for the official celebrations called for a solemn Mass in the Holy Ghost Church, then a festive parade from the church to the *Hofbräuhaus* on November 3, 1997. All the *Stammgäste* were requested to march in the parade along with over two hundred bands from all over Bavaria. Special medallions were minted commemorating the event sold for DM 40 to all members (and DM 50 to the general public). The management held a special poetry contest online and the winner of the competition received a special gift from the *Hofbräuhaus* gift-shop. The brewery produced a special "*Jubiläumsbier*" for the occasion. The *Hofbräuhaus* expected to sell one liter of the special brew for every day of the past one hundred years: 36, 525 liters of beer. The selling price for the special beer was DM 4, about six marks cheaper than normal.[13]

If the *Hofbräuhaus* had become a symbol for Bavarian culture in Germany, then by the 1990s the *Hofbräuhaus* became a symbol of Bavarian culture throughout the world. The nineties marked the beginning of a *Hofbräuhaus* offensive in export. This represented a cultural export offensive as well. The *Hofbräuhaus* insisted that its beer, and also its food, be prepared in accordance with strict Bavarian recipes. The reason thousands of tourists flocked to the beer hall in Munich every year was that it represented authentic, "old world" Bavarian culture. When the tourists returned home they still wanted to experience that Bavarian *gemütlichkeit* without having to make the pilgrimage to Munich. Beginning in 1988 *Hofbräuhaus* beer concessions began to appear in all parts of the world. In that year a *Hofbräuhaus* beer hall opened in Tokyo, Japan under license from *Hofbräuhaus* Munich. Shortly thereafter a *Hofbräuhaus* beer hall appeared in Thailand. All of these beer halls had to comply with the strict requirements of *Hofbräuhaus* regulations, or they lost the right to use the name.

The task of remaining the "world's most famous beer hall" and defending the quality of the product has not been easy. In the 1980s the beer industry in Bavaria became threatened by all kinds of lawsuits in the European courts. Non-Bavarian brewers sued over the practice of excluding beers not brewed according to the beer purity law from the Bavarian market. In 1984 the European Supreme Court ruled that the Bavarian practice represented "restraint of trade" and therefore unconstitutional. Bavarian brewers, however, vowed that they "won't let anyone spit in our beer." Therefore, even though today other, non-Bavarian brands of beer can sell in Munich and Bavaria, the big five brewers still brew their beer according to the 1516 beer purity law.[14] In 1989 the directors of the major breweries signed a public pledge, renewing their commitment to the beer purity law of 1516. Most of the major breweries brew the beer in Munich and have resisted attempted takeovers. Even when foreign companies have purchased breweries in the city, the beer is still made in the city and according to the purity requirements. To this day only the five major beers brewed within the city can be sold at the Oktoberfest. And when that beer festival is not in session, the *Hofbräuhaus am Platzl* is still the place to experience Oktoberfest fun and Bavarian *gemütlichkeit* all year round. This is why it is still the number one tourist destination in Europe to this day.[15]

Globalization has taken its toll on the Munich beer industry as well. Accordingly, the concessions at the World Cup games of 2006, some of which will be held in Munich, will serve Anheuser-Bush (American!) beer.[16] One wonders if Bavarians will drink it, for as this book has hopefully demonstrated, Bavarians and the citizens of Munich take their beer very seriously.

In fact, in 1992 a "Beer Garden Revolution" erupted. When people living near the "Waldwirtschaft" beer garden complained of too much noise, the Munich Administrative Court ordered that the beer garden close a half-hour earlier (before 11:00PM) and be closed on at least two Sunday evenings of every month. This is one of Munich's most famous and popular beer gardens, and the court's decision threatened *Müncheners* ability to relax after a hard day. In summer 1995, after various appeals failed to get the verdict overturned, 25,000 angry *Müncheners* stormed the *Marienplatz* in front of City Hall, demanding the politicians do something. The protestors eventually succeeded in getting the ruling overturned and beer gardens remained open until 11:30PM. Today the "revolution continues." Several cities in Germany have extended the hours for pubs and beer halls to be open later, until midnight. Munich and Bavaria are expected to follow, and allow beer halls and beer gardens to be open until midnight, rather than close at 11:30PM. (During the World Cup Soccer Tournaments held in Munich in 2006, the city will experiment with allowing beer gardens to remain open until midnight).[17]

Other revolts and protests made 1992 truly a "revolutionary" year in Munich. In addition to the "Beer Garden Revolution" another revolution of sorts occurred: a massive city-wide protest against racism and prejudice. Responding to racist violence against foreigners throughout Germany, on December 6, four-hundred thousand *Müncheners* joined in a candlelight protest throughout the city. Forming a human chain in rows sometimes five people deep, the chain stretched through all the streets and squares in Munich, including the little square in front of the *Hofbräuhaus*. Church bells rang during the demonstration held on St. Nicholas Day, and German and foreign newspapers recorded that they had never seen a stronger protest against prejudice and anti-foreigner hatred anywhere.[18]

By 1997, the company planned to open a *Hofbräuhaus* restaurant in Cincinnati Ohio, which is a "sister city" to Munich. Built just outside Cincinnati, in Newport Kentucky, a twenty minute's drive from Cincinnati Airport, beer is brewed right on the premises according to the Bavarian beer purity standards. And, while the restaurant offers traditional Bavarian fare such as *Schweinshaxe* and *Jagerschnitzel,* it also offers American steaks, barbeque ribs and "Spicy Cajan Pasta." In 2001 the company announced plans to open the first *Hofbräuhaus* replica in Las Vegas, Nevada. The *Hofbräuhaus* Las Vegas is a scale replica of the great room of the *schwemme* in Munich, and the exterior of the building is modeled on Bavarian neo-Renaissance style, the first such *Hofbräuhaus* replica building anywhere in the world. Here the beer is shipped to Las Vegas, and even the pretzel ingredients are imported from Munich. The cook and many of the staff at one time worked in the *Hofbräuhaus am Platzl*. Even the bands in Las Vegas are from Germany. The *Hofbräuhaus* Las Vegas has attracted a local following. According to the Gastager brothers, who own and operate the franchise, only forty percent of the customers are tourists; sixty percent are local and regular customers. "The Americans who live here want something real–and that's what we give them." Even the mugs are imported from Germany.[19] The success of these establishments testify to the popularity of Bavarian culture and the beer hall atmosphere found in the *Hofbräuhaus*, even for those who have never been to Munich. What Coca-Cola and Pepsi are for the United States, *Hofbräuhaus* beer is for Munich and Bavaria: a symbol of Bavarian culture found throughout the world.

In a very rare occurrence for the *Hofbräuhaus*, the cavernous beer hall went silent on the afternoon of September 11, 2001. On that day, the day when hijacked planes were used to destroy the World Trade Center in New York, and the Pentagon in Washington DC and murder almost 3000 people, no music played in the famous *schwemme*. Out of shock, and out of respect for the many dead, and in solidarity with the United States, all of Munich seemed to remain silent that day in September. All over the city during the next several days, moments of silence, prayer services, and observances were held by the people of Munich, trying in small ways to express their support for the American people.[20]

The terrorists attacks in New York and Washington DC effected the *Hofbräuhaus* as tourism declined drastically. Americans, fearful of air travel, stopped traveling to Europe; some have not been on a plane since. Only recently has the tide turned. In fact, tourism in Munich generally is reported to be up for the first time in three years. In the first six months of 2004, tourism was up 7.9%. Of this group the largest number of visitors were Americans. With 113,000 visitors, Americans replaced Italians as the largest tourist group to visit Munich.[21]

Munich has become a diverse city, a metropolis. In fact, there is an ongoing debate as to whether or not the city ought to allow skyscrapers to be erected to increase business and housing space. Critics have protested bitterly that buildings should not be built any higher than Munich's churches, which create the unique skyline of the city. The critics argue that they might as well change the name of the city to "Muc-York" or "Munchhatten" if it were to loose its distinct skyline.[22] Nevertheless, the city continues to welcome visitors from all over the world even as it tries to reposition itself for the twenty-first century.

And doubtless the *Hofbräuhaus* will continue to adapt to the new times while at the same time retaining its Bavarian tradition and *gemütlichkeit.* Today, the *schwemme* can seat about 1,300 people. In total, the *Hofbräuhaus* Munich holds 3,000 people inside and 500 people in the beer garden. There are over 100 *stammtische* and over 5000 registered *stammgäste.* In July 2004, and after a long and arduous search, the Sperger brothers Michael and Wolfgang were named the new managers of the *Hofbräuhaus am Platzl.* The *Hofbräuhaus* manager position is renewed every five years. Michael and Wolfgang Sperger were the favorite choice of the *stammgäste* as well. Beer sales and business have doubled under the Sperger family leadership. After their father, Michael died in 2000, the two brothers took over the management with their mother Gerda, who decided to retire in 2004.[23] They in turn have had their problems. In 2004 a scandal broke out over the working conditions of waiters and waitresses in the world's most famous beer hall. The Spergers used an employment agency to supply them with servers. According to agency regulations, their employees could be terminated with or without cause or reason, they would be docked a half-hours wages for being even slightly late, they were not allowed free food while working, and in some instances they were not paid while they were being trained. Some, including the Bavarian Association for Restaurants and Gastronomy, termed it "modern day slavery." The Sperger brothers only hired the employment agency and had no idea about the adverse conditions of the employees' contracts with the agency. The Spergers agreed to pay back wages and salary to all workers and trainees.[24]

Despite these ups and downs, the *Hofbräuhaus* remains the most popular tourist destination in Germany. In fact, perhaps a little too popular. In 1994 an American sociology student from New Mexico was stopped for trying to smuggle out a mug with the famous "HB" symbol on it. The mug can be bought in any souvenir store or even in the *Hofbräuhaus* itself for about $20.00. The student was then arrested, and spent four weeks in jail while Bavarian judicial authorities sorted out the mess. In the end, the District Court of Munich released him after he paid a 1260. euro fine.[25]

Some in the Bavarian government have also had the *Hofbräuhaus* in their sights. Eike Hallitzky, a member of the Green Party, is only the latest politician to argue that the *Hofbräuhaus* should be privately owned. "Beer brewing is not one of the original responsibilities of the state" he declared recently, and proposed that the *Hofbräuhaus* be privatized. "The *Hofbräuhaus* will not be sold!" responded Bavaria's Finance Minister, Kurt Faltlhauser in a dispute that spilled over into the newspapers.[26]

More than a "sacred cow," the *Hofbräuhaus* has come to represent Munich and Bavarian culture to the world, probably as much as the famous Oktoberfest. The brewery just opened a new restaurant in the new "Terminal

Two" of Munich's Franz-Josef Strauss airport. Therefore, in many cases, the first thing travelers see when they enter or leave Germany through Munich is the famous "HB" symbol. It is one of Germany's most enduring marketing symbols, and evidence of its fascinating history. And that symbol is recognized world wide: in 2005 the "Superbrands" corporation voted the "HB" symbol one of the most recognized symbols in the world. Headquartered in London, "Superbrands" is an international organization that seeks to identify quality companies throughout the world. Addidas athletic wear is another such quality firm singled out by "Superbrands."[27]

Munich served as a host city for the 2006 World Soccer (World Cup) Tournament that began with the Germany vs. Ecuador match on June 9, 2006. Nine million tourists came to Munich during the World Cup tournament. Spanish television *Univision* based its broadcast coverage of the games in Munich. The city built a huge, new "state-of the-art" stadium to host the games: The Allianz Arena. Completed in May 2005, the Allianz Arena replaced the 1972 Olympic Stadium as the home of Munich's championship-caliber soccer teams: *F.C.Bayern-Munich*, and *Munich 1860*.[28]

Could the *Hofbräuhaus* cope with such an international event? Easily! Every day the *Hofbräuhaus* serves enough beer to surround an entire soccer field with liter steins. Each year, the *Hofbräuhaus* serves enough dumplings to fill an entire soccer stadium. The *Hofbräuhaus*, and all of Munich's beer halls and beer gardens, became "foreign embassies" where visitors from all over the world met and interacted with the locals. Though many governments, including the United States, issued warnings to tourists to watch-out for "hooliganism," violence from fans, and prostitutes, few serious incidents of crime were evident. Despite the dire predictions, there was little if any vandalism: beer, bratwurst, and soccer seemed to be most in demand. And even though Bavarian police noted an increase in licensed sex workers flocking into Munich before the games, the brothels, legal in Germany, did particularly poor business during the games.[29] More importantly, however, the World Cup games illuminated several important changes that have taken place in Germany and Munich since reunification in 1990.

The games suggest that, sixteen years after the fall of the Berlin Wall and the reunification of the two Germanies, reintegration of the German people has reached a milestone. For the past sixteen years, Germans have been divided by a psychological "Wall in the Mind" (*Mauer im Kopf*): Germans from the West lamented the cost of reunification, while Germans from the East resented the patronizing attitude of their Western countrymen. But in 2005 Germans elected Dr. Angela Merkel Chancellor of Germany. She is not only the first woman ever to hold the Chancellorship; she is also the first Eastern German (from Leipzig) elected to nation-wide office since reunification. Moreover, several of the best players on the German World Cup team were from the Eastern zones of the country. Michael Ballack, the team's captain and a star player, was born in "Karl Marx-Stadt," Chemnitz today. At the games, no one referred to the players or the fans as "*Ossies*" or "*Wessies,*" they were simply Germans playing on the national team and the country was clearly united behind them. These developments suggest that the psychological wall that separated Eastern and Western Germans since political reunification in 1990 may have finally been breached.[30]

That Germans viewed the team and its efforts as a truly national endeavor is without question. Throughout the World Cup event, which lasted a full month, Germans displayed, for the first time since 1945, a "normal nationalism" exhibiting the national colors everywhere. Indeed, the black-red-gold tricolor, dating from the Wars of Liberation from Napoleon, and the democratic Revolutions of 1848, seemed ubiquitous during and after the conclusion of the games. The flag hung from houses and businesses, shops and stores; it flew from cars and bicycles, government buildings and apartments. And at the tournament, hundreds of thousands of flags were to be seen in the overfilled stands; fans painted their bodies and face in the national colors and cheered the team forward with shouts of "Deutschland!" Still, the obnoxious xenophobia that usually accompanied German nationalism before 1945 was absent. Even the English soccer fans, prone to taunt Germans with reminders of the war, were impressed with the new confident yet welcoming atmosphere in Germany. The soccer competition appears to have provided a venue to express admiration for the team and pride in the nation, without threatening anyone.[31]

On April 19, 2005 Munich received an indirect, though nevertheless important honor. The former Archbishop of Munich and Freising, Josef Cardinal Ratzinger, became Pope Benedict XVI. Ratzinger served as Archbishop in Munich from 1977 to 1982 before moving to Rome under Pope John Paul II as the Prefect of the Congregation for the Doctrine of the Faith. The first German pope in over one thousand years is a Bavarian from Munich. Despite the city's sometimes troubling history, Munich remains the "city of good feeling" in Germany and the old time *gemütlichkeit* can still be found in its many beer halls and festivals to this day. Munich is, as its slogan maintains, "A Cosmopolitan City with a Heart," a *"Weltstadt mit Herz."* And the heart of that city still beats in the *Hofbräuhaus am Platzl.*

Notes

Introduction: *Munich*: Hofbräuhaus *and History*

1. See David Clay Large, *Where Ghosts Walked: Munich's Road to the Third Reich.*
    (New York, 1997), p. xii-xiii.
2. See for example, James J. Sheehan, *German History 1770–1866.* (Oxford, 1989);
    see also the companion to this volume by Gordon A. Craig, *Germany,
    1866–1945* (Oxford, 1978). For a very fine comprehensive history of Germany
    in one volume (in English) see Steven Ozment, *A Mighty Fortress: A New History of the German People* (New York, 2004).
3. David Clay Large, *Berlin.* (New York, 2000); see also Anthony Beevor, *The Fall
    of Berlin: 1945,* (New York, 2002); Anonymous, with translation by Philip
    Boehm, *A Woman in Berlin: Eight Weeks in the Conquered City* (New York,
    2005).
4. David Clay Large, *Where Ghosts Walked: Munich's Road to the Third Reich.* The
    Large book offers us a rich context in which to observe the development of the
    Nazi movement. The Rosenfeld book illuminates Munich's seeming attempts to
    cover up its past during the period of reconstruction. See Gavriel Rosenfeld,
    Munich and Memory (Berkeley, 2000).
5. See Robert Eben Sackett, *Popular Entertainment, Class, and Politics in Munich,
    1900–1923* (Cambridge, 1982). George Bailey, *Munich* (Amsterdam, The
    Netherlands, 1980).
6. Recently, a three volume chronicle of the city's history has appeared in German
    and these volumes cover only the sixteenth through the nineteenth centuries.
    See Helmuth Stahleder & Richard Bauer, *Chronik der Stadt München* (Munich,
    2005).
7. See, for example, Beate Kümin and B. Ann Tlusty (eds.), *The World of the Tavern: Public Houses in Early Modern Europe* (Aldershot, 2002); *B. Ann Tlusty,
    Bacchus and Civil Disorder: The Culture of Drink in Early Modern Germany*
    (Virginia, 2001); Susanne Rau and Gerd Schwerhoff (eds.), *Zwischen Gotteshaus
    und Taverne: Öffentliche Räume in Spätmittelalter und Früher Neuzeit. Norm*

und Struktur: Studien zum sozialen Wandel in Mittelalter und Früher Neuzeit, Band 21 (Cologne, 2004).

8. David Clay Large has written of the live-and-let-live atmosphere of Munich's beer hall culture. He has also noted that the beer hall could be a very rowdy place, with frequent brawls and fights. He charts the beer hall culture, and Munich's transition from a city of good nature to the headquarters of the Hitler movement in *Where Ghosts Walked*, pp. xii–xiii.

9. There is some controversy regarding Munich's reconstruction: some have argued that by rebuilding the city to its pre-1945 appearance, Müncheners were trying to erase or cover up its connection to the Nazi past. Some argue that Munich existed long before the Nazis and exists today despite the twelve year Nazi regime, and that the city should have been rebuilt as close to the original city as possible. The controversy is well covered in Gavriel Rosenfeld, *Munich and Memory* (Berkeley, 2000).

1.   Religion, Politics and Beer: The Origins of Munich's Hofbräuhaus

1. Further removed by the invading Germanic tribes, the Celts eventually went to Gaul (France) and later to the British Isles. See George Reichlmayr and Rudolf Ites (ed.) *München, Eine kürzer Stadtgeschichte* (Erfurt, 2001), p.10.

2. Charlemagne deposed the Agilolfinger family and awarded Bavaria to several Germanic yet non-Bavarian rulers. By the twelfth century, the Holy Roman Emperor made these awards to his vassals. See Reichlmayr & Ites, p. 11.

3. See Fritz Fenzl, *Münchener Stadtgeschichte* (Munich, 2004), pp.14–18.

4. Franz Trautmann, *Legends and Tales of Old Munich* (Munich, 1958), p. 11.

5. Klaus Brantl, *Strahlendes München* (Munich, 1960), p. 5.

6. See Reichlmayr and Ites, pp. 10–13. Some scholars have pointed out that there is little evidence that a monk settlement was even there, but that Henry said there was to bolster his case for a new city. Whatever settlement was there, Henry turned it into a merchant town by 1158, presenting the Holy Roman Emperor with a *fait accompli*. See also Richard Bauer, et al., *Geschichte der Stadt Münchens* (Munich, 1972), pp. 16–18.

7. Otto, Frederick's spy at Henry's court, was a Bavarian and so the rule of Bavaria returned to a native family for the first time since Charlemagne. See Reichlmayer & Ites, p. 17. The province of Austria, which had been part of Bavaria before Henry, remained a separate entity. See the intricate politics of the Holy Roman Emperor in Alfred Haverkamp, *Medieval Germany 1056–1273* (Oxford, 1992), p. 263.

8. See the *Festschrift for the 350ᵗʰ Anniversary of the Hofbräuhaus Munich* (Munich, Hofbräuhausamt, 1939), pp. 29–30.

9. Italian names like Perusa, Ruffini, and Maffei are common in Munich even today. For the Italian influence in Munich, see Brantl, p. 14. For Munich's Jewish roots and their significant contributions to the city's commerce, see Bauer *Geschichte Münchens* (Munich, 2003), p. 33.

10. Reichlmayr & Ites, pp. 20–21. Sometimes the earliest flags and crests of the city were black and gold field with lions, since these animals were at one time common to the area around the *Hofbräuhaus* and old city. See Brantl, p. 14; and

Fenzl, p. 16. The fires are described in Fenzl, pp. 36–37; for the reign of Ludwig der Bayer see Bauer et al., *Geschichte der Stadt München*, pp. 61–62.

11. See Philip Ziegler, *The Black Death* (New York, 1969), pp.66–67. Pigs were often allowed to roam throughout the city to eat the offal thrown into the streets. Fenzl points out that sanitation in the city was less than thorough. See Fenzl, pp. 41–49. Even though many citizens of Oberammergau had already succumbed, the city suffered less victims than other cities in the area. The play, too, included elements of anti-Semitism that were only removed for the 2000 performance. The 2000 text (in English and German) is found in *Passionspiel 2000* (Oberammergau, 2000). For the controversy surrounding the play, see James Shapiro, *Oberammergau: The Troubling Story of the World's Most Famous Passion Play* (New York, 2000).

12. Horst Dornbusch, *Prost! The Story of German Beer* (Boulder, 1997), pp. 40–42.

13. "Von Michaeli bis zum Georgen." Through the summer months the beer would have to be "lagered" or stored in basements or "kellers" to keep it cool and fresh for consumption during the summer months. Dornbusch, p. 47.

14. History of the beer purity law is recorded in the *400th Anniversary Festschrift of the Hofbräuhaus Munich* (Munich, Gerber Verlag, 1989), pp. 36–38.

15. See Brantl, p. 15; and Bauer, *Geschichte Münchens*, p. 47.

16. Reichlmayr & Ites, p. 30.

17. See Horst Dornbusch, *Prost! The Story of German Beer*, pp. 66–67.

18. The events of the Reformation and the "revolutionary" aspects of the movement are well described in Steven Ozment: *Protestants: The Birth of a Revolution* (New York, 1991), pp. 13–19.

19. Luther was responding to the "Twelve Articles of the Peasants of Swabia" the written declaration of the revolutionary peasants. Luther declared that the peasants and their leaders had seriously misunderstood the Gospel. He declared that even Abraham and the Patriarchs had slaves and that, in the words of St. Paul, slaves should obey their masters. In his second pamphlet, he declared that nothing could be more dangerous, "hurtful, or devilish than a rebel." See Eugene F. Rice, *The Foundations of Early Modern Europe* (New York, 1970), pp. 150–152.

20. Some Lutherans fled to Augsburg and Nuremberg and, at least in the case of the latter, the city became protestant. See Bauer, *Geschichte Münchens*, p. 55; The Munich Lutherans were generally wealthy, so that lots of money and commerce also left the city. See Fenzl, pp. 84–85. Whereas St. Benno is the patron saint of the city, the Virgin Mary is the patron saint of Bavaria. See Reichlmayr & Ites, p. 35.

21. For example, beer became 30% more expensive for each 100 kilometers it was shipped. That meant that, by the time beer reached Munich from Hannover, Einbeck cost three times its original price. *HB Festschrift*, p.20.

22. The famous mechanical clock in Munich's City Hall is a representation of the Marriage of Wilhelm V to Renata von Lothringen which took place on 21 February 1568. See Fenzl, p. 87. The poem is recorded in Paul Brandt, p. 20.

23. 350th Festschrift, p. 11.The cost estimate was 1, 477 guilders. By 1591 Munich's Hofbräuhaus had already started a hearty, dark-brown beer.

24. In the middle ages the church allowed monks to have five servings of beer per day. These servings were usually measured out as between one and two liters each. The word for measure ("zumessungen") became known as a Maß, and the

word is still used today in Bavaria for a liter stein of beer. See *Der Biercomic: Die Geschichte vom Hofbräuhaus in München,* Birgit und Rainer Stock, (Munich/Rottach, 2004), p. 21.

25. 350th Anniversary Festschrift, pp. 12–15.

26. 1 bucket of beer equaled 64 liters or 17 gallons of beer. See Brandt, p. 20.

27. See Larry Hawthorne, *The Beer Drinker's Guide to Munich* 4th Edition (Honolulu, 2000), p. 80; see also *www.hofbraeuhaus.de,* "1610" and "1614" on the brewery "history" web page.

28. Rice, pp. 162–164. As a result of their support of the Roman Church and the Holy Roman Emperor, Bavarian Dukes gained permission to direct the clergy in Bavaria, visit monasteries and remove abbots, priests and bishops, and limited permission to tax the clergy.

29. Richard S. Dunn, *The Age of Religious Wars, 1559–1715* (New York, 1979), pp. 65–66.

30. See Dunn, pp. 84–86.

31. Carl J. Friedrich, *The Age of the Baroque* 1610–1660 (New York, 1952), pp. 179–183.

32. Gustav's sight-seeing is recorded in Bauer, *Geschichte Münchens,* p. 70.

33. 220 hectoliters equaled about 5, 812 gallons. See Brandt, p. 72. In addition, the Swedes took 42 Munich citizens hostage to ensure payment. Most of these hostages returned to the city in April 1635 when the Swedes were forced to retreat after a counterstrike by Wallenstein's army in Franconia in September 1632. See Richard Bauer (Ed.), *Geschichte der Stadt München* (Munich, 1992).

34. See Bauer, *Geschichte der Stadt München,* p. 209.

35. See Fenzl, p. 82; Reichlmayr & Ites, p. 35.

36. See Reichlmayr & Ites, p. 47.

37. See Dunn, p. 65. To understand the religious transformation in Germany at this time, see Gordon A. Craig, *The Germans* (New York, 1983), pp. 83–103.

38. At least this is Dornbusch's contention. See Dornbusch, p. 66. The early seventeenth century is sometimes referred to as the "little ice age" because several of the years were so cold and rainy, even in summer. See "Augsburgs Tavern Keepers" in Tlusty, *Bacchus and Civil Disorder,* p. 38.

2. *From Occupation to* Oktoberfest: *Munich becomes a World City, 1715–1828*

1. See Friedrich Prinz, *Die Geschichte Bayerns* (Munich, 1997), p. 279.

2. See T.R. Reid's article "Caffeine" in *National Geographic Magazine,* January 2005, pp. 3–32. Boiling water to make coffee or tea killed the bacteria and germs in the water (which was one of the reasons so many people drank mostly beer up until this time), p. 15.

3. See Prinz, *Geschichte Bayerns,* pp. 279–280. By 1720 the "Kurfürst's Fabrik" employed 2000 people. By 1747 a cotton factory on the outskirts of the city employed 5000 people, and the duke's porcelain factory was founded in 1755.

4. "Statistics of Munich" recorded by Johann Pezzl and cited in *München: Ein Lesebuch,* edited by Reinhold Bauer (Frankfurt/Main, 1986), pp. 22–23.

5. As we saw in the last chapter, after the age of religious wars, some of the most beautiful churches were erected in Munich. In the early eighteenth century, the Asam bothers built their beautiful churches in the city, and St. Michael's Church and the Cajetan Brothers Church were erected in this period. See Prinz, *Geschichte Bayerns,* p. 287.

6. Founded by Adam Weishaupt (1748–1830) the *Illuminati* organization spread to all parts of Germany. See Prinz, *Geschichte Bayerns,* pp. 289–290.

7. See Bauer, *Geschichte Münchens,* p. 91.

8. Rumford, who became a leading man of science in his retirement years, died near Paris in 1814. See "Rumford and Kultur" by R. M. Manley in the *New York Times,* March 7, 1915, p. x10. In the colonies Rumford is remembered as the brutal commandant of the "King's American Dragoons" that occupied Huntington Long Island briefly in 1782. See "The Man Huntington Loved to Hate" by George De Wan in *Long Island, Our Story* (New York, *Newsday,* 1998), p. 133.

9. See Fenzl, *Münchener Stadtgeschichten* (Munich, 2004), pp.153–155.

10. "Unter all den Städten." By W.A. Mozart, cited in *München: Ein Lesebuch,* p. 15.

11. According to the author Robert Gutman, the Archbishop of Salzburg, by whom Mozart was already employed, probably sabotaged Mozart's chances with the Elector of Bavaria so as to keep him in Salzburg. By March 1781 Mozart had left Munich for good. See Gutman's very fine biography, *Mozart: A Cultural Biography* (New York 1991), pp.491–502; 526–527. See also Stanley Sadie's biography in the "New Grove" series of biographies *Mozart* (New York, 1982), pp. 74–77. See also Baily, p. 82.

12. See Fenzl, p. 151. Reichelmayr and Ites argue that with Mozart and the newly completed Cuvilliés theater, Munich would have rivaled Vienna in the world of Music. See p. 51.

13. See Reichlmayr and Ites, p. 59. St. Matthew's was also the center of Protestant opposition to the Nazi regime in the 1930s. In 1938, under orders from the Gauleiter of Bavaria Adolf Wagener, the church was destroyed in order to broaden the street (as part of Nazi plans to rebuild the city but also to crush that opposition). The church was rebuilt after the war and remains directly opposite the Sendlinger Gate today. See Bauer (ed.), *München: Ein Lesebuch,* pp. 265–267.

14. Cited in George Bailey, *Munich* (Amsterdam: Time-Life Books, 1980), pp. 53–56. Rumford had even invented a cheap soup of Barley and potatoes to feed the poor of Munich. Even to this day the soup is known as *Rumfordsuppe.*

15. At the time of the First World War, there were still Washingtons fighting in the Austrian army. See "Baron George Washington Fighting for Austria," in the *New York Times,* September 3, 1916, p. sm14. Baron Jacobus' second son, Charles remained in Bavarian service and later served as Chamberlain to Ludwig II.

16. Richard Bauer (ed.), *Geschichte der Stadt Munchen.* (Munich, 1992), pp. 263–266.

17. Reichlmayr and Ites, pp. 60–61.

18. This made the political unification of Germany, Otto von Bismarcks achievement in 1870–1871, much easier. See Prinz, *Geschichte Bayerns,* p. 300.

19. Many of the religious objects confiscated, ended up in the museums Maximillian now ordered erected, the thousands of books seized became part of the new Bavarian State Library. See James J. Sheehan, *German History, 1770–1866* (Oxford, 1989), pp. 262–269.

20. The occupation of Bavaria is recounted in Bauer, *Geschichte der Stadt München;* p. 265.

21. The events of the French occupation of Germany are well covered in Sheehan, *German History: 1770–1866,* pp. 255–263. The Cardinal Archbishop of Munich is the highest Roman bishop in Bavaria. The creation of the new archdiocese is recorded in Bauer (ed.), *München: Ein Lesebuch,* p. 388.

22. Places like Weihanstefan, the famous cloister brewery near Freising which bills itself as the oldest continuous brewery in the world, was taken over by the Wittelsbach's personally and converted into an agricultural institute which later became the Royal Bavarian Academie. Today it is the beer brewing institute of the Technical University of Munich. See Birgit Eckelt, *Biergeschichte(n)* (Rosenheim: 1999), pp. 18–45.

23. Recorded in the 350th Anniversary *Festschrift,* p. 19.

24. The *Bockbierkeller* was on the spot where the Platzl Bühne theater (now Planet Hollywood) once stood. See Cornelia Oelwein, *Das Münchener Platzl* (Munich, 2003), p. 7; 37–38.

25. See Eckelt, *Biergeschichte(n),* p. 84.

26. According to Prinz, *Geschichte Bayerns,* pp. 316–317. On the happy atmosphere and the various classes of people to visit the beer hall, see Jules Huret's observations in Bauer (ed.), *München: Ein Lesebuch,* p. 116.

27. Demand for *Hofbräuhaus* beer was so great that on the outskirts of the old city a storage annex was established, the *Hofbräuhauskeller* on the Wienerplatz. Before it became a restaurant later in the nineteenth century, it was used to store reserve amounts of beer. See Fenzl, pp. 142–144. Even when the "bierkeller" was no longer necessary thanks to modern refrigeration, breweries competed with each other to provide the nicest beer garden which quickly became a Bavarian tradition. See below, chapter 4.

28. Ernst von Destouches, "Die Gründung des Oktoberfestes 1810" cited in Bauer, *München: Ein Lesebuch,* p. 28. Actually, the date of the Oktoberfest was changed in the late nineteenth century to late September, early October because of the weather: October can be very cold and rainy in Munich.

29. The observer, Nudelmüller, is recorded in Eckelt *Biergeschichte(n),* p. 41.

30. On the very first day of the festival, the brewers and directors of Oktoberfest parade through the streets of Munich, at least since 1887. Information on the history of Oktoberfest and the national costume can be found in the *Oktoberfest Munchen 2004 Festprogramm,* pp. 8–19 "Die Geschichte der Lederhos'n." See also Franz Gieshofer, *Die Lederhose* (Husum/Munich, 1996), pp. 110–111.

31. Figures according to Larry Hawthorne, *The Beer Drinker's Guide to Munich,* 4th Edition (Honolulu, 2000), p. 180.

32. Reichlmayr and Ites, pp. 62–63.

33. See Sheehan, pp. 413–414. See also Reichlmayr and Ites, p. 63.

34. See Brigitte Huber (ed.). *Tagebuch der Stadt München* (Ebenhausen, 2004), p. 15.

35. This information is taken from a series run in the Munich *Tageszeitung,* 9 January, 2001. It was accessed via the HB web site at www.hofbraeu-muenchen.de/news/tz

3. *The Reign of the Ludwigs: 1828–1897*

1. See Henry Channon, *The Ludwigs of Bavaria* (London, 1952), pp. 31–32.
2. Reichlmayr and Ites, p. 66.
3. This is the testimony of an eye witness cited in Paul Brandt, *Das Münchener Hofbräuhaus* (Munich, 1997), p. 25. Prior to 1828 the *Hofbräuhaus* was essentially a beer making factory where people were allowed to drink. After 1828, the brewery was slowly becoming a restaurant.
4. The Hofbräuhaus 350th Anniversary *Festschrift* has a lot of this information (p. 20). See also Horstmann's recollections in *Consular Reminiscences* (Philadelphia, 1886), pp. 199–200.
5. See Hawthorne, p. 18.
6. See Larry Hawthorne's *The Beer Drinkers' Guide to Munich* (Honolulu, 1995), p. 22. Horstmann cites the micro brewery figure in his *Consular Reminiscences* and claims that there were only 2,500 breweries in the USA. See pp. 334–335.
7. Today the *Maderbräu* is the *Weissesbräuhaus* on the Tal, across from the Holy Ghost Church. The rioters even stopped to pray silently when the bells of the Holy Ghost Church rang the hour. As soon as the bells had stopped, patrons picked up their mugs and continued the destruction. The stories are recorded in Eckelt, *Biergeschichte(n),* p. 83–89.
8. See Brandt, pp. 25–27.
9. Cited in Eckelt, p. 88.
10. See Prinz, *Geschichte Bayerns,* pp. 364–373. See also Reichlmayer and Ites, p. 70.
11. The King eventually had her portrait added to his *Schönheitsgalerie* ("Gallery of Beauties"), a collection of paintings of the most beautiful women he could find. The portraits, including Lola's, are now held in Nymphenburg Castle. See Channon, pp-42-46. Whether this really happened is still debated. Nevertheless it is clear that the king became obsessed with Lola and increasingly showered her with favors. See Bruce Seymour, *Lola Montez, A Life* (New Haven, 1996), pp. 102–105.
12. When not in the company of the king or "performing" she was often in the company of young University students, some of whom now formed a fraternity, the "Alemania" which served as her private body guard as she walked the streets of Munich. *Müncheners* referred to them as "Lola's Harem." See Bruce Seymour, *Lola Montez, A Life,* pp. 107–110; 142–150.
13. See Sheehan, pp. 660–661, 703–710; on the Lola episode, see Bruce Seymour, *Lola Montez, A Life,* pp. 107–110; 142–150.
14. Birgit Eckelt, *Biergeschichte(n),* p. 85.
15. Channon, pp. 50–55. See also Eckelt's stories of the King's mistress in *Biergeschichte(n),* pp. 68 & 91.
16. The Cholera epidemic of 1853 even claimed Ludwig I's wife, the former Queen, as a casualty. See Reichlmayr and Ites, pp. 69–74.

17. See Brandt, 27.
18. Heyse's observations are recorded in Paul Brandt's book on the *Hofbräuhaus,* pp. 72–73. Wolfe's famous description of the *Hofbräuhaus* is found in his novel *The Web and the Rock* (New York, 1938), pp. 661.
19. According to Reichlmayr and Ites, p. 68.
20. All in an attempt to preserve native Bavarian culture and traditions, as well as the unique history of Bavaria within a larger Germany. See Prinz, *Geschichte Bayerns,* pp. 370–371.
21. Desmond Chapman-Houston, *Ludwig II: The Mad King of Bavaria* (New York 1993), pp. 57–58.
22. Ludwig held out the possibility of social and professional stability. See Channon, pp. 62–64. Chamberlain-Houston, p. 62.
23. See Robert W. Gutman, *Richard Wagner: The Man, His Mind, and His Music.* (New York, 1990), pp. 239–256.
24. The *Wagner Festspiel* is run by descendants of the master to this day. See Chapman-Houston, p. 195. See also Reichlmayr and Ites, pp. 78–79.
25. See Channon, p. 77.
26. The Jesuits and Redemptorist orders had already been exiled from Bavaria, the Jesuits as early as 1773 since these orders were seen as hostile to the reform movement in Bavaria at this time. Still, Bismarck insisted that Roman Catholic Schools and Seminaries be monitored. In addition extra confessional and secular schools were established for the first time See Prinz, *Geschichte Bayerns,* pp. 392–393. By 1876 one-third of all Catholic parishes in Prussia alone had no priest as they were either arrested or driven out of the country. All monastic orders except those providing medical services, had been outlawed. See Gordon A. Craig, *Germany 1866–1945* (Oxford, 1978), pp. 69–76.
27. See Peter Krückmann *The Land of Ludwig II* (Munich, 2003), a tourist book which recounts the history of all of Ludwig's grand creations.
28. Cited in Channon, p. 77. The kings brother, Otto, was already in a straight jacket and held essentially under house arrest for his own protection. The Castle *Herrenchiemsee,* which Ludwig built to rival the Palace of Versailles on a beautiful island in southern Bavaria, was probably the most expensive palace ever built up to that time and almost caused the county's fiscal collapse. It was never finished. See Channon, pp. 101–104.
29. See Desmond Chapman-Houston, pp. 279–289. Charles von Washington was a great-grandson of James Washington and George Washington's great-great uncle.
30. This is how the Hofbräuhaus 350th Anniversary *Festschrift* describes the effects of unification on the brewery's prospects. See the *Festschrift,* p. 20.
31. The average tip was five cents. The story is described in G. Henry Horstmann, *Consular Reminiscences,* pp. 17–18; 201.
32. "Nymphenburger Strasse has a Long and Colorful History" by Michele Owen, *Munich Found,* # 8; vol. XVIII, October 2005, p. 40.
33. Brandt, p. 27. The trade mark information is from the *www.hofbraeuhaus.de* web site.

4. *The "Golden Years" of Munich: 1897–1918*

1. Information on the transformation of the *Hofbräuhaus* can be found in the *400. Jahre Hofbräuhaus Festschrift*. See pages 38, 64, 159. See also the *Hofbräuhaus* internet site, www.hofbraeuhaus.de.

2. The emergence of the large beer halls also represented the extent to which beer had become a lucrative business by the 1890s. The transformation of the "beer culture" is well described in *Wirtshäuser in München um 1900* (Munich: Buchendorfer Verlag, 1997), pp. 9, 23–35, p. 61. The city also experienced an explosion of vegetarian restaurants, automat-cafeterias, cafes and tea houses in the same period. See pages 101–132.

3. It is now a multiplex cinema. See Cornelia Oelwein-Baumann, *Der Orlandblock am Münchener Platzl* (Munich, 2000), pp. 75–77; on Orlando di Lasso see pp. 9–35.

4. Before refrigeration, brewing was done only during the cooler months from September to April. The beer was stored in cellars and sold throughout the summmer in gardens attached to the breweries. See *Wirthäuser*, pp. 28–41.

5. *Wirtshäuser in München um 1900*, pp. 22–50. Gemütlichkeit is a hard word to translate but will be familiar to anyone who has been in the *Hofbräuhaus*, had one or two *maß* beer, and joked around with people from all over the world. Gemütlichkeit can mean "hospitality," "friendship," and fun all at the same time. A general "good time."

6. See *1897–1997: Ein Hundert Jahre Hofbräuhaus*, p. 50; the art form of the beer hall waitress is discussed in *Wirtshäuser*, p. 203. The *Hofbräuhaus* waitress (and today waiters) still astound customers with the number of beer steins they are able to hold in one hand, sometimes as many as six (2 hands = 12 liter mugs!) Without spilling a drop.

7. See Bauer, *Geschichte Münchens*, pp. 126–127, & Bauer, *Geschichte der Stadt Münchens*, pp. 312–313; Albert Einstein lived in Munich during this period of scientific renaissance. See Reichlmayr and Ites, pp. 86–87.

8. *Wirtshäuser*, pp. 81–83. In 1868 there were fifteen private breweries, forty by 1880, and only 25 by 1900. The "six" breweries are really four today: Spatenbräu and Löwenbräu are owned by the same company today, and in 1984 Paulaner bought Hacker-Pschorr Bräu. Larry Hawthorne's *Beer Drinker's Guide to Munich*, 5th Edition (California, 2005) is a wonderful resource for short histories and customs of all of Munich's major and minor beer halls. See especially pp. 28–33.

9. Brandt, *Hofbräuhaus*, p. 113.

10. See LaVerne Ripley, *The German Americans* (Boston, 1976), p. 76. Between 1830–1930 six million Germans found their way to the United States. Emigration was more intense in times of "high economic activity" and not necessarily when economic times were bad. See Mack Walker, *Germany and the Emigration 1816–1885* (Cambridge/Harvard, 1964), pp. 181–183.

11. One could not walk from the Karl's Gate to the *Hofbräuhaus* without being accosted by beggars or prostitutes. See Large, pp. xviii–xx.

12. Prinz, *Geschichte Bayerns*, p. 414. By 1912, the Social Democratic Party became the largest party in the German (National) Reichstag. See Craig, 291–294.

13. See Eckelt, *Biergeschichte(n)*, pp. 69–70; 101–103. Also helpful regarding the beer strikes and demonstrations is the *Münchener Stadtchronik* (www.muenchen. de/rathaus/dir/stadtarchiv/chronik). See also Brigitte Huber (ed.), *Tagebuch der Stadt München* (Munich, 2004).

14. Weiß Ferdl and Sepp Eringer were regular performers between 1931–1944, but almost all the famous Bavarian folk-singers made their way across the Platzl stage. *Platzl Bühne: Festschrift 85 Jahren* (Munich, 1991).

15. Unfortunately today the Platzl Bühne is now a "Planet Hollywood." See Robert Eben Sackett's impressive study of the Volksänger: *Popular Entertainment, Class, and Politics in Munich, 1900–1923* (Cambridge, 1982), pp. 11, 43, 54–66.

16. "A Cheer, A Cheer to Good Times" Ein Prosit der Gemütlichkeit is a toast known to any visitor to the beer hall or Oktoberfest. The sketch implies that in the *Hofbräuhaus* there is no north or south, east or west, and the place is totally unique, as is perhaps Bavaria. Weiß Ferdl "Nord und Süd im Hofbräuhaus." Of course the sketch also meant that Bavarian culture trumped all others. Sound recording: *Weiss Ferdl's Linie 8* (Munich BMG/Ariola Media, 1991).

17. *Wirtshäuser*, p165. The *Stammtisch* was usually denoted by a sign hanging over the table. These were usually ornate and painted and God help the person who sat at the table when they were not permitted. After World War II, as the tourism industry exploded, the *Hofbräuhaus* added personal lockers for member steins to prevent tourists from stealing them from the cupboards.

18. Birgit Eckelt, *Biergeschichte(n)*, pp. 103–104.

19.   "Hier finden sich auf brüderlichem Bänken
        Hoch und Gering in traulichem Gemische:
        Den knechten nah, die seine Pferde lenken,
        Der Staatenlenker vom Ministertische;
        Pedell, Professor, Famulus, Student-
        Du spülst hinweg die Schranke, die sie trennt."
Paul von Heyse "Ode auf das Hofbräubier, recorded in *1897–1997 100 Jahre Hofbräuhaus am Platzl*, p. 34. A Berliner invited to Munich by Maximillian II, Heyse was known as the "master of the novelle." and won the Nobel Prize for Literature in 1910. See also the *400 Jahre Festschrift*, p. 53.

20. See Eckelt, p. 81–98.

21. Scholars have noted that several of the revolutionaries of 1848 were regular *stammtisch* visitors. Today the *Hofbräuhaus* has over 100 *Stammtische*. See "Die Wiege der Revolution" in Munich's *Abendzeitung*. 5/6 September 1998, p. 3. Of course since politics was regularly discussed, it was not uncommon for the government to plant spies in the beer hall as well. See *Wirtshäuser*, p. 157. This was Hitler's occupation in 1919: military spy to the beer halls.

22. Ludwig Thoma, *An Angel from Munich* (Munich, 1988). From the German *"Der Münchner im Himmel."* Hingerl, failed to deliver his message because he could not get past the *Hofbräuhaus*.

23. In the period 1886–1890, beer consumption equaled 487 liters per person per year; 1909 255 liters, and in 1911 320 liters per person per annum. See, Michael Schattenhofer, *München, 1870–1910* (Frankfurt/Main, 1980), pp. 3–11.

24. For the history of electric light in Munich, see "Das Licht geht an- die Geschichte der Straßenbeleuchtung in München" published by the Lan-

deshauptstadt München, October, 2004. For Einstein's early years and his scientific productivity, see David Cassidy, *Einstein and Our World* (New York, 2004, 2nd Edition), p. 24. See also, "Munich Celebrates 100 Years of Einstein's Brilliance" by Victoria Owen in *Munich Found*, #8, vol. XVIII, October 2005; p. 37.

25. See Birgit Eckelt, *Biergeschichte(n)*, pp. 108–109. On Lenin see Reichlmayr and Ites, pp. 87–88.

26. The *Gemütlichkeit* and excitement belied an undercurrent of class tension and economic pressures building before World War I, which all came to a climax after 1918. See Sackett, p. 5.

27. Mandlinger died a few weeks before the end of World War II. He reportedly lost the will to live when the *Hofbräuhaus* was destroyed by bombs in April 1945. "Now they have taken my means of existence away, I've got nothing left." His picture hung in the Stadelheim room of the *Hofbräuhaus* until recently. The Stadelheim room was converted to the gift shop in 2004/2005. See Brandt, p. 115.

28. Famous visitors to the *Hofbräuhaus* are discussed in all the works published by the Hofbräuhaus. Ibsen and Wedekind are also mentioned in Schattenhofer, *München: 1870–1910* (Frankfurt/Main, 1980) p. 4; and the *Tageszeitung*, 10 January 2001 (www.hofbraeuhaus.de) respectively.

29. See Reichlmayr and Ites, pp. 88–89.

30. See Large, p. 4. By 1890 Schwabing had grown as famous as Monmartre and Paris as a European art city. In 1890, Schwabing, with a population of over 11,000 people, was incorporated into the city of Munich. See Baily, p. 112. On Kandinsky see also, Robert Bersson, *Worlds of Art* (London, 1991), pp. 398–399.

31. The vitality and freedom that attracted so many to Munich could be found nowhere else in Germany. Schwabing afforded an "intellectual gemutlichkeit" not unlike the beer hall culture in other parts of town. See Bailey, pp. 119–120.

32. Puppets too, were used to represent the European powers and mock international events and some of these puppets can be seen in the city museum today. See Bauer (ed). *München, Ein Lesebuch*, pp. 125–126. See also Mary M. Paddock, "Redemption Songs or How Frank Wedekind set the Simplicissimus Affair to a Different Tune." in the German Studies Review, #2, vol. XXVIII, May 2005; pp. 245–264.

33. Weiß Ferdl too lamented "Cohen and Sara" racing around the city in their motorcar. Cited in David Clay Large, "Ghosts," pp. xxii–xxiii.

34. "Rise in Food Cost Arouses Germany," the *New York Times*, September 1, 1912, p. C1.

35. Large, pp. 48–49. On the *Burgfrieden*, and those heady days of 1914, see Craig, *Germany 1866–1945*, pp. 340–341.

36. See Anton Joachimsthaler, *Hitler's weg begann in München* (Munich, 2000), p. 81.

37. Hitler's first reactions to Munich recorded in *Mein Kampf* (New York, 1971) translated by Ralf Mannheim, pp. 126–127.

38. Above all, Hitler saw Munich as the quintessential German city. See Large, p. 39.

39. See Joachimsthaler, pp. 77–78. Hitler's roommate was one Rudolf Häusler with whom he lived for about 9 months. His land lady at the time, Anna Popp, remembers only one letter from a sister in Vienna.

40. Joachimsthaler, pp. 83–86. Later, after Hitler became Chancellor, these paintings sold for several times their value. A teacher from Ingolstadt, Friedrich Echinger, sold several paintings to the NSDAP archives for RM 5000. a piece, by far the best art investment Echinger ever made.

41. Joachimsthaler, p. 89. If Joachimsthaler is correct, Hitler probably earned about RM100. a month from painting, but paid only RM20. for rent. In 1913, a typical Munich worker, says Joachimsthaler, earned about RM96–116 a month with a family to support.

42. Joachimsthaler, pp. 88–89. The *Hofbräuhaus* was apparently a favorite subject. According to Joachimsthaler, if one adds up all the time Hitler needed to paint then sell so many pictures, he probably had very little time for anything else, including hanging around in coffee houses talking politics, as he would later claim took up much of his time.

43. The charge was leveled by Munich brewers protesting the rationing of hops. See Large, pp. 58–64.

44. "Beer Drought in Munich," *New York Times,* June 18, 1915, p. 18.

45. Munich's Beer Prices Held Down" *New York Times,* December 30, 1915, p. 3; "Brewing to be Cut Again" *New York Times,* January 27, 1916, p. 3. The state had by now taken over the production and distribution of food stuffs and ordered rationing. In many places lemonade was served instead of beer. See Bauer, *München,* pp. 336–344.

46. "Wounded in Munich Riots" *New York Times,* June 21, 1916, p. 5.

47. Eckelt, *Biergeschichte(n)*, pp. 107–108.

48. See Large, pp. 58–63. See also Bauer, *Geschichte der Stadt München,* p. 342.

49. "Germany's Hunger Told in Her Press." *New York Times,* May 27, 1917, p. 34; Increase of Tuberculosis and Many Epidemics of Stomach Troubles." *New York Times,* February 24, 1918, p. 43.

50. "Turns Foods into Powder" *New York Times,* May 14, 1916, p. xii; "Says Germans want a Stomach Peace" *New York Times,* June 15, 1918, p 2. See also Bauer, *München,* pp. 338–342.

51. The exploits of Captain Beauchamp are recorded in the *New York Times:* "Flies 435 Miles in Raid on Munich, Lands in Italy" November 18, 1916, p. 1; "Threw Six Bombs in Raid on Munich" November 20, 1916, p. 3; "Bombed Kaiser's House" December 20, 1916, p. 4. Beauchamp died in combat in December 1918.

52. See Rilke's observations in Bauer & Piper (eds) *München/Lesebuch,* p. 169–170.

53. Of these women, only 19.5% had ever worked in a factory before. The figures are cited in David Large, pp. 58–65. See also Prinz, *Die Geschichte Bayerns,* p. 405. For World War I casualty figures, see Reichlmayer and Ites, pp. 92–93.

54. *Wirtshäuser,* pp. 52–53.

5. *Chaos Theory: Revolutionary Munich*

1. See Reichlmeyr and Ites, p. 93; Bauer, *Geschichte Münchens,* p. 139.

2. Allan Mitchell, *Revolution in Bavaria 1918–1919: The Eisner Regime and the Soviet Republic.* (Princeton, 1965), pp. 100–103.

3. Large, p. 79. When the king realized that his security forces would no longer protect him, the royal family fled first to Wildenwarth and then out of the country. See also Bauer, *Geschichte Münchens,* p. 139.

4. In the elections of January 1919, Eisner received less than 2% of the total vote. See R.G.L. Waite, *Vanguard of Nazism: The Free Corps Movement in Postwar Germany 1918–1923* (New York, 1952), p. 81.

5. Mitchell, p. 275.

6. Mitchell, pp. 286–304.

7. Conditions described in Waite, "Vanguard," p. 84. See also Waite, *Psychopathic God: Adolf Hitler* (New York, 1977), pp. 206–207.

8. See Waite "Vanguard," pp. 84–85.

9. Mitchell, p. 324.

10. Waite, p. 87.

11. Toller's description cited in Richard Grunberger, *Red Rising in Bavaria* (London, 1973). p. 123. See also Mitchell, pp. 325–327.

12. Mitchell, pp. 324–325.

13. Waite, p. 84.

14. For Heisenberg see Cassidy, *Uncertainty The Life and Science of Werner Heisenberg* (New York, 1991), p. 57; For Hitler, see Adolf Hitler, *Mein Kampf* (Boston, 1971), p. 208.

15. This is the final verse from Ferdl's *Das Revoluzerlied* ["The Revolter Song"], and is cited in Robert Eben Sackett *Popular Entertainment, Class and Politics in Munich, 1900–1923* (Cambridge, 1982), p. 99. Some suggest that this is why he "acquiesced" in Nazi "misdeeds" in World War Two. See Grunberger, "Red Rising," pp. 155–156.

16. Waite, p. 88. See Lenin's admonitions to the revolutionary leadership in Grunberger, "Red Rising," pp. 156–157. See also David Clay Large, *The Politics of Law and Order: A History of the Bavarian Einwohnerwehr, 1918–1921* (Philadelphia, 1980), p. 15.

17. The terror of the "White Reaction" is well recorded in Friedrich Hitzer's *Der Mord im Hofbräuhaus* (Frankfurt/Main, 1981). On the Perlach murders, for which the murderers faced no punishment, see pp. 197–207.

18. The quote belongs to Karl Schwend, a Bavarian historian writing about the revolution in the 1950s. Cited in Large, the *Politics of Law and Order,* p. 8.

19. All of Hitler's early socialist activities were suppressed by the regime so thoroughly, that it has taken years to recover the truth. The most current research on the issue is Anton Joachimsthaler and Ian Kershaw, *Hitler: 1889–1936 "Hubris"* (New York: W.W. Norton, 1999). See also Ronald Hayman, *Hitler and Geli* (London and New York, 1997), especially pages 54–55.

20. This is the Joachimsthaler argument. See Joachimstaler, pp. 201–202.

21. Joachimsthaler insists that it was his experience in the revolution, combined with his military intelligence training in 1919 that truly formed Hitler's political beliefs. If Hitler had a world view in 1919, says Joachimsthaler, it was probably semi-leftist, having been elected a *Vertrauensmann* of the demobilization battalion/2nd infantry Regiment in February 1919. Joachimsthaler insists that Hitler could not have been elected to that position unless he expressed definite

SPD/Socialist convictions since the soldiers and the government were revolutionary. See Joachimsthaler, pp. 177–188. On Jewish influx into Munich see pp. 246–247.

22. According to the directive of the Bavarian War Ministry of 6 August 1914, Austrians of draft age were to be delivered to the border police for military service in Austria. See *München: Hauptstadt der Bewegung*. Wolfgang Till (ed.), Munich 1993, p. 22.

23. Ian Kershaw, *Hitler: 1889–1936* "Hubris" (New York: W.W. Norton, 1999). For Hitler's gradual entrance into Bavarian politics, pp. 120–127; for Hitler's comments, see *Mein Kampf,* p. 219.

24. Brian Deming and Ted Iliff, *Hitler and Munich* (Berchtesgaden, 1980), p. 11

25. The meeting occurred in November 1919. See Large, p. 133.

26. Joachimsthaler, pp. 268–269.

27. See the description in Large, p. 135.

28. See Hitler's description in *Mein Kampf,* p. 369. The *Festsaal* of the *Hofbräuhaus* can hold up to 2,000 people.

29. Ian Kershaw, *Hitler: 1889–1936* "Hubris," p. 147.

30. Joachimsthaler, pp. 271–273. Some of the largest beer halls in Munich aside from the *Hofbräuhaus* included the *Bürgerbräu, Münchener-Kindlkeller, Matthäser Bierstadt, Hackerbräu, Wagnerbräu* and the *Löwenbräukeller.*

31. As Ian Kershaw has written, it was less *what* he said than *how* and when he said it. The message struck a cord in postwar Germans that it had never struck before. See Kershaw, "Hubris" pp. 132–133.

32. Kershaw discusses this issue at length. See Kershaw, "Hubris" pp. 160–165.

33. Joachimsthaler, pp. 292–297.

34. Deming and Iliff, p. 11.

35. Kershaw, "Hubris" p. 152.

36. See Large, p. 148.

37. Recorded in Kershaw, "Hubris," pp. 175–176.

38. Joachimsthaler, p. 307: the *"Vereignigten Vaterländischen Verbänden Bayerns."*

39. Kershaw suggests, therefore, that the whole personality cult of "Der Führer was born in the *Hofbräuhaus am Platzl.* See Kershaw, "Hubris," p. 180.

40. Kershaw, "Hubris," pp. 190–191.

41. Of course Mussolini copied the salute from the Roman army and the *fasci,* the private body guards of the Roman Emperors. See Kersahw, "Hubris" p. 193.

42. See Kershaw, "Hubris" pp. 190–201. By November 1933 printing houses had to keep 1,783 presses open around the clock to produce the amount of currency needed. See Craig, Germany *1866–1945,* p. 450.

43. Gradual at first, the inflation exploded into hyper-inflation by October/November 1923. In July 1919 that same liter of beer cost 40 pfennigs, July 1920, RM 1,20; August 1922, RM 14; July 14, 1923, RM 9,000; August 29, RM 280,000, October 6, RM 18,500,000; November 9, RM 72,800,000; November 16, RM 140 billion, See Brandt, pp. 94–95.

44. *HB 400. Jahre Festschrift,* p. 163. In 1914 $1.00US was equal to $4 German Reichmarks.

45. The situation was actually quite dangerous and could have become deadly, if not for Hitler and the putschists' bungling. See Harold J. Gordon, *Hitler and the Beer Hall Putsch* (Princeton, 1972), pp. 283–292; pp. 314–335.

46. Von Kahr, General Otto von Lossow head of the Reichswehr, and Colonel Hans von Seisser head of the Bavarian police formed a sort of conservative dictatorship in Bavaria. Later that evening, Ludendorff released them on their "word of honor." The events are recorded in John Dornberg, *Munich 1923: The Story of Hitler's First Grab for Power* (New York, 1982), pp. 68–90.

47. Weiß Ferdl cited in Robert Eben Sackett, pp. 99–100. See also Large, p. 193. For the "Law for the Protection of the Republic," see, Gerhard F. Kramer, "The Influence of National Socialism on the Courts of Justice and the Police" in *The Third Reich* (New York, 1975); pp. 603–604. Ludendorff faded out of the Nazi movement after this period, but Göring followed the leader almost up to the very end as chief of the Gestapo and *Reichsmarshall* in charge of the air force. See also Dornberg, pp. 248–315.

48. Helmut K. Anheier and Friedhelm Neithardt, "The Nazi Party and Its Capital: An Analysis of the NSDAP Membership in Munich, 1925–1930." *American Behavioral Scientist,* June–July 1998, vol. 41, No. 9, p. 1219. See also Kershaw, "Hubris" p. 266.

49. Large, "Ghosts" p. 221.

50. Figures cited in Large, "Ghosts," pp. 221–224.

51. The quote is Theodor Lessing's. Cited in Richard Grunberger, *The Twelve Year Reich* (New York, 1971), p. 3. "The Satyricon" (1969) is Frederico Fellini's famous film on the reign of the Roman Emperor Nero.

6. *The "New Order"*

1. See Craig *Germany 1866–1945,* pp. 569–570. Papen expressed confidence that he could control Hitler.

2. *Trials of the Major War Criminals before the International Military Tribunal at Nuremberg,* "The United States vs. Josef Altstoetter, et al." vol. III; (Washington, U.S. Government Printing Office, 1951), pp.160–161. Under Article 48 of the Weimar Constitution, the President could pass emergency decrees under the State of Emergency. Unfortunately, he signed almost anything Hitler put under his nose, especially after the fire. On the reorganization of the court system, and the laws subverting justice, See Jeffrey Gaab, *Justice Delayed: the Restoration of Justice In Bavaria under American Occupation 1945–1949* (New York, 1999), pp. 26–31.

3. See *München Hauptstadt der Bewegung,* pp. 196–199. For the way the regime consolidated Germany under their control (*Gleichschaltung*) see Martin Broszat, et al. (ed.), *Bayern in der NS-Zeit,* volume 3, pp. 513–567 (p. 542). See also volume 4, pp. 384–433.

4. By the end of March the first fatalities were recorded. At least 31,591 prisoners would die at Dachau, 30,000 survivors were liberated by American forces in 1945. When originally opened, the camp had room for only 1100 prisoners. See *München, Hauptstadt der Bewegung,* pp. 235–250.

5. Cited in Huber (ed.), *Tagebuch der Stadt München,* p. 121.

6. By April 1934 Hitler had promised to deal with the Brown Shirt problem at his earliest opportunity. See Large, "*Ghosts,*" p. 251.

7. Among the dead were also three women, including the wife of General von Schleicher. See *München, Hauptstadt der Bewegung*, p. 228. For the events leading up to the murders in Munich, see David Clay Large, *Where Ghosts Walked*, pp. 250–251.

8. See Gordon Craig, *The Germans*, p. 8–9.

9. Mayer died in Munich in 1948. Mayer had served as a chaplain in World War One, and had lost a leg due to his service. Mayer was the first Roman Catholic chaplain in Germany to receive the Iron Cross, 1st Class. One of his most ardent followers was the young attorney Otto Gritschneder who the Nazis refused to issue a law license because of his affiliations with Mayer. See Otto Gritschneder in Karl Denk, *Der Selige Pater Rupert Mayer, S.J.* (Munich, 1987). See also Large's discussion in *Where Ghosts Walked*, pp. 295–297.

10. Here again Gritschneder serves as an eye witness. See Gritschneder, *Kardinal Michael von Faulhaber zwischen Widerstand und Anpassung.* (Munich, 1978).

11. The observations are by Ernest Pope, the US Reuters News Service correspondent who lived in Munich in the 1930s. See Ernest R. Pope, *Munich Playground* (New York, 1953); pp. 243–245.

12. There are several essays on drinking in the Third Reich. See Geoffrey J. Giles, "Student Drinking in the Third Reich," and Hermann Fahrenkrug, "Alcohol and the State in Nazi Germany." Both essays found in Susanna Barrows and Robin Room, *Drinking: Behavior and Belief in Modern History* (Los Angeles, 1991).

13. Bauer, *Geschichte der Stadt Munchen*, p. 379. See also Bauer, *München Ein Lesebuch*, p. 395. On the "Day of German Art" see Robert Wistrich, *Weekend in Munich* (London, 1995), pp. 10–12.

14. After the war, the gallery was used as display for modern art, the very art Hitler despised. In 1992 a "Pinokothek der Moderne" modern art museum opened in Schwabing. There has been talk of tearing down the "Haus der Kunst" but so far no action has been taken. See Large, 231–232 and 256. See also *München Wie Geplant* (Munich, 2004); p. 94; and

15. Recorded in Bauer, *Geschichte der Stadt München*, pp. 377–378.

16. The restaurant is still there today known as the "Osteria Italiana." Speer's eyewitness account is recorded in Bauer, *München: Ein Lesebuch*, pp. 237–239; 272–273.

17. Brandt has the date wrong as April 24. See Brandt, pp. 97–98.

18. See Large, p. 276.

19. Pope describes the scandal in *Munich Playground*, pp. 173–174. The episode is briefly mentioned also in Brandt who says that Bacherl gave Esser "a thrashing" which "won him a great deal of sympathy from the [Munich] population." See Brandt, pp. 99–100.

20.   In Munich stands a Hofbräuhaus,
                 one, two, drink!
                 they sell out so many little barrels of beer,
                 one two, drink!
                 Many brave men have been there
                 one, two, drink!
                 to see how much they could try,
                 early in the morning they begin

and come out only late at night
because it's so nice in the Hofbräuhaus!
The *Hofbräuhaus* Song by Wiga Gabriel is cited in *400. Jahre Hofbrauhaus Festschrift*, p. 232.

21.   On Lindbergh's affair with the Hesshaimer sisters, see *Sueddeutsche Zeitung*, 6 August 2003. For Lindbergh and the royalty, see Large, *Ghosts*, p. 277. On Kennedy, see Nigel Hamilton, *John F. Kennedy: Reckless Youth* (New York, 1992). In one visit Kennedy and friends got into a scuffle with local brown shirts for not reverencing a shrine to Horst Wessel, the Nazi martyr. See pp. 191–268

22.   See Thomas Wolfe, *The Web and the Rock* (New York, 1937). See especially chapters 46–48; pp. 650–680. The chapter on the Oktoberfest was also published in *Scribners Magazine* as "Oktoberfest" (Vol. 101, # 6; 1937) pp. 27–31.

23.   The Czechs, and their Soviet allies, were not even invited to the conference. See Telford Taylor, *Munich: The Price of Peace.* (New York, 1979). Hitler was very disappointed by the peace celebrations of "his Müncheners" since he wanted war, he wanted them to want war too. See Bauer, *Geschichte der Stadt München,* pp. 390–391. See also Craig, pp. 667–671.

24.   See Huber (ed.) *Tagebuch der Stadt München*, pp. 126–128. The gradual destruction of Munich's Jewish community is recorded in Angelika Baumann and Andreas Heusler (ed.), *München Arisiert: Entrechtung und Enteignung der Juden in der NS-Zeit* (Munich, 2004).

25.   See Angelika Baumann and Andreas Heusler (ed.), *München Arisiert,* see especially pp. 38–49.

26.   The T4 Program and medical killing is very well covered in Robert J. Lifton, *The Nazi Doctors: Medical Killing and the Psychology of Genocide (New York, 1986),* pp. 71 & 93.

27.   For the Hitler speeches, see Kershaw, "Nemesis," pp. 436; 538–539; 606; and 739.

7.   *From World War to* Weltstadt, *1939–1958*

1.   Bavaud was executed in Plötzensee Prison in 1941. The regime tried to claim that Elser was working for the British but, despite much torture, he never claimed that anyone else was involved in the assassination attempt. He was executed at Dachau on 9 April 1945. For a complete discussion of the many attempts on Hitler's life, see Peter Steinbach and Johannes Tuchel (eds.) *Lexikon des Widerstandes 1933–1945* (Munich, 1994), pp. 13–49.

2.   The episode is recorded in Large, "Ghosts," p. 322.

3.   All of the members of the White Rose were tried for treason before the famous "Peoples' Court and executed. See Fenzl, pp. 204–205. See also Inge Scholl, *The White Rose, Munich 1942–1943* (Connecticut, 1983).

4.   Stauffenberg had tried to kill Hitler at least twice before the July attempt. All or most of the conspirators were arrested and executed (hanged by piano wire in Plötzensee Prison near Berlin). Field Marshall Erwin Rommel, associated with the plot, was forced to commit suicide. See Peter Hoffmann, *The History of the German Resistance 1933–1945* (Cambridge, 1977), pp. 373–503.

5.   The speech and the scene are recorded in Ian Kershaw, *Hitler 1936–1945 "Nemisis,"* pp. 623–624.

6.   See Large, p. 340 and Kershaw "Nemisis" p. 781. This was Hitler's last public statement to the German people.

7.   See Brandt, p. 98. See also Large "Ghosts" pp. 342–347. The *Bürgerbräu* material is recorded in "Munich is in Ruins: Nazi Shrines Fall" New York Times, May 2, 1945, p. 12. On the history of the *Löwenbräukeller*, see the www site: loewenbraeukeller.com.

8.   "Uprisings Sweep South of Reich" *New York Times,* April 29, 1945, p. 10. By noon that day the city was again in the hands of the SS. See, Bauer, *Geschichte der Stadt München,* p. 393.

9.   "No Officials left to Give Up Munich." *New York Times,* May 1, 1945, p. 7.

10. Hans Bacherl had kept the beer hall running almost up to the last days of the war, when only the tap room remained usable. See Brandt, pp. 98–100.

11. "Tanks Clog Roads in Push on Munich." *New York Times,* April 30, 1945, p. 3.

12. Lutz Niethammer, "Die Amerikanische Besatzungsmacht zwischen Verwaltungstradition und Politischen Parteien in Bayern, 1945" in the *Vierteljahrshefte für Zeitgeschichte,* 15 (1967): 153–210; p. 177.

13. "Munich in Ruins; Nazi Shrines Fall," *New York Times,* May 2, 1945; p. 12. In fact his name was Eugene Keller Jr.

14. Douglas Botting, *From the Ruins of the Reich* (New York, 1985). pp. 195–196. See also Wolfgang Malenowski (ed.), 1945: *Deutschland im Stunde Null* (Hamburg, 1985), pp. 19–20.

15. Prinz & Krauss, pp. 8–9.

16. See the *New York Times,* 26 April 1959, p. 26: "Munich Restored, Bigger than Ever."

17. These figures are cited in David Clay Large, *Where Ghosts Walked,* p. 346.

18. These are figures cited by Botting. Civilians in Britain received about 2,800 calories a day, German farmers 3000, and American G. I.s about 4,200. Botting writes that a "House of Commons Select Committee" estimated that "a diet of 1,200 calories a day may be characterized as slow starvation . . . 1,550 calories is probably no better." Botting, pp. 130–135.

19. The ban on beer was lifted as soon as it was clear that there would be enough bread for the winter. See Large, p. 351 and also Prinz & Krauss, p. 107.

20. "Vom Besatzer Zum gerne Gesehenen Gast: Die Amis kommen!" in the Munich *Tages Zeitung* (Online), 11 November 2001.

21. See Hajo Holborn, *A History of Modern Germany* (Princeton, 1969), vol. 1; p. 53.

22. "Conquest's Meaning Dawns on Germans" in the *New York Times.* May 15, 1945; p. 4.

23. Justus Fürstenau, *Entnazifizierung* (Neuwied/Berlin 1969), pp. 24–26.

24. See Fürstenau, pp. 26–27.

25. Cited in Beata Ruhm von Oppen (ed.), *Documents on Germany under Occupation,* 1945–1954 (New York, 1955), p. 17.

26. Ruhm von Oppen, pp. 19–20.

27. In 1955 it was estimated that there were approximately 66,730 illegitimate children in West Germany; 37,000 of whom had American fathers. Among these fathers, 10% were African-American. Figures are recorded in Fruhstorfer,

Georg and Heidi, *Hurra, Wir Leben Noch! München nach 1945.* (Gundersberg/München, 2003), p. 30.

28. Or at least that's how the newspapers reported it. The controversy demonstrates that, in the early days after World War II, the Germans and Americans had a hard time finding anyone to work for them that did not have a Nazi past. For the Schaeffer controversy, see Fritz Baer, *Die Minister-Präsidenten Bayerns* (Munich, 1971), pp. 13–16. For the Patton Affair, see Ladislas Farago, *Patton: Ordeal and Triumph* (New York, 1963), p. 777.

29. Hoegner, a lawyer, also served concurrently as Minister of Justice. He began the arduous task of purging and rebuilding the legal system in Bavaria. See Gaab, *Justice Delayed*, p. 45.

30. "Law for the Liberation from National Socialism and Militarism of 5 March 1946," (Ministerium für Sonderaufgaben, Munich, 1946), Articles Three and Four.

31. "Liberation Law," article 23/ Chapter II.

32. "Liberation Law," Articles 24–25.

33. Karl Loewenstein, "The Reconstruction of Justice in Germany" *Harvard Law Review,* 61 (1948), p. 451

34. *Stadtchronik der Stadt München* (www.muenchen.de/rathaus/dir/stadtarchiv/chronik) October 2004 "1946." Ferdl claimed that he never used the Heil Hitler! greeting, but many remembered his skit from the early years of the regime. Meschugge in Yiddish sounds better than the same word in German translation, which means "cracked" or "crazy."

35. Friedrich Prinz (ed.), *Trümmerzeit in München* (Munich, 1984); p. 343.

36. The Allies used what had been the concentration camp facilities at Dachau to hold former SS Guards and other Nazis for trial but had built other barracks for refugees. See "Expellees on Strike: Competing Victimization Discourses and the Dachau Refugee Camp Protest Movement, 1948–1949" by Brenda Melendy in the *German Studies Review,* vol. XXVIII, # 1, February 2005; pp. 107–126.

37. The currency reform, the economic merger, as well as the move toward political unity in the West, led the USSR to begin reconstituting their zone of occupation as the "German Democratic Republic" or East Germany, by October 1945. See Henry A. Turner, *Germany from Partition to Reunification* (New Haven, 1992), pp. 22–29.

38. Bonn was viewed as a provisional capital: temporary until the country could be reunited once again. See H.A.Turner, *Germany from Partition to Reunification* (New Haven, 1992), pp. 35–40.

39. See George Marek, *Richard Strauss: The Life of a Non-Hero* (New York, 1967), especially pp. 270–298. On Fiehler see the Stadtchronik, 14 January 1949. Fiehler had been in jail since the end of the war.

40. Recorded in the *Stadtchronik der Stadt München,* 1946–1949. The Office of Nutrition and Economics brought charges against the management of the *Hofbräuhaus* for serving beer with between 12.5 and 12.8 % real beer as *"Märzenbier."* at Oktoberfest. According to the charges, beer less than13% real beer could not be marketed as "March Beer" (*Märzenbier*) which is heavier than regular beer. See also Huber (ed) *Tagebuch der Stadt München,* p. 147; and Fruhstorfer, pp.15–17. Thomas Wimmer is also the one who began the tradition of

the Munich Mayor tapping the first barrel of beer at the opening of Oktoberfest with the words "O' zapft es" ("It's tapped!").

41.   See Rudi Dix, *München, Das waren die Fünfziger* (Munich/Berlin, 1994), p. 95.

42.   For the stewardship of Valentine Emmert and the 1951 fire, see Brandt, pp. 101–103.

43.   In fact, the hope of future tourism influenced the decision to restore the Old Town center of Munich to its traditional appearance rather than try and rebuild it along modern lines. See Bauer, p. 403–404. This has caused some historical controversy: some have argued that by restoring Munich to its prewar form was an attempt to cover up and "forget" the Nazi experience. The controversy is well covered in Gavriel Rosenfeld, *Munich and Memory* (Berkeley, 2000).

44.   In total 16 oxen and 240,000 chickens had been consumed demonstrating that Munich's food industry had finally recovered from the war. 751 wallets, 70 wristwatches, 150 purses, two dogs, 1,100 key sets, 241 children, 3 sets of false teeth, and 5 sets of rosary beads were lost. One assumes that at least the children were returned to their owners. Recorded in the *Stadtchronik der Stadt München* (online) "October, 1951."

45.   On the *"Verein gegen betrüglisches Einschenken"* as it was known in German, see Brandt, pp. 91–92. The *Verein* was reestablished in 1970, and in 1984 was successful in getting most breweries to use glass mugs, so that checking the amount of beer in a mug became much easier. See the *Verein's* history on its web site (Vgbe.de). The Trimborn affair is recorded in Dix *München: Das waren die Fünfiziger*, pp. 11–12. See Kirschner (ed.), *1897–1997: 100 Jahre Hofbräuhaus*, pp. 44–45.

46.   Even to this day, the *Hofbräuhaus* adheres strictly to the beer purity standards of 1516, as do all the breweries in Bavaria. Even the food in these establishments must be genuine. *Müncheners* simply would not tolerate anything less. The controversy is mentioned in press articles from the period (1956) assembled in the *Staatsarchiv München*, "Hofbräuhaus München" folder # 11.

47.   On 15 December 1957 Thomas Seehaus of Pasing was born, Munich's one millionth citizen. See Bauer, p. 413.

48.   Recorded in Large, p. 208–210. She danced regularly in Berlin, however and that may be why Munich banned her. The "Hofbräuhaus Lenbach" mentioned in chapter four, painted her portrait on one of her visits to the *Hofbräuhaus*. See Brandt, pp. 114–115. Her visit to Munich in 1950 is recorded in the *Stadtchronik der Stadt München* (online) "1950."

49.   Even though the *Hofbräuhaus* Song was written and first performed in 1939, it really became famous in the 1950s, especially as more and more tourists, famous and not so famous, visited the city. Recorded in press articles assembled in the Staatsarchiv München, Hofbräuhaus München folder # 11.

8.   *The Most Famous Beer Hall, the Most Popular City*

1.   Mozart's *Ideomeno* might have been more appropriate since he wrote the opera in the city, but still it was a miracle that the breathtaking Cuvillies Theater was rebuilt in time for the ceremonies. See the coverage of the events in "Munich to

Mark 800th Birthday" in *The New York Times,* June 1, 1958, p. 27. See "Munich Acclaims 800th Birthday" in *The New York Times,* June 15, 1958, p. 11.

2. Cited in Large, p. 359.

3. Munich's Olympic Park and Stadium complex is built on one such "hill." (See below). See "Modern Miracle Made in Germany" in *National Geographic Magazine,* vol. CXV, No. 6. June 1959, pp. 735–791.

4. Of course the city fathers had tourism on their minds as well and figured that tourists would be more drawn to the city if it looked like Germany and not just another modern metropolis. See Gavriel D. Rosenfeld, *Munich and Memory* (Berkeley, 2000), pp. 23–41.

5. See Prinz, *Geschichte Bayerns,* pp. 514–517.

6. "Modern Miracle" in *National Geographic Magazine,* June 1959, p. 738–744.

7. "A New Twist to Munich's Night Life" in the *New York Times* Travel Section, June 14, 1964 p. x37.

8. American influences on Bavarian popular culture are cited in Bauer, *Geschichte Münchens,* p. 212.

9. The *Mathäser Bierstadt* finally closed its doors in 1992, the site is now a cinema. *Staatsarchiv München,* Hofbräuhaus München, folder # 11.

10. Harold Schonberg's observations in *The New York Times,* "Munich: Art and Boom" August 26 1961, p. 2, col. 3.

11. The renovations of the 1960s and 1970s are briefly mentioned in the *Hofbräuhaus 1897–1997,* pp. 52–54; and the *Hofbräuhaus 400. Jahre Festschrift,* p. 96.

12. Bauer, et al.; *Geschichte der Stadt München,* pp. 413–415. Vogel already had plans to campaign to have the summer 1972 Olympic games in Munich. That would require almost a total reworking of the city's infrastructure.

13. What caused all the violence? It was after all, just a simple disturbing the peace report. See Fenzl, pp. 241–243. In 1968, students in Munich occupied the offices of the *Bild Zeitung* Press. In the scuffles with police that ensued, two were killed. See Reichlmayr and Ites, p. 118.

14. See Brandt, p. 105. This also demonstrates the persistence of the *Hofbräuhaus'* popularity with American military personnel since 1945.

15. Craig covers the creation of the *Bundeswehr* in *The Germans,* pp. 242–243. For the protests in Munich, see John Dornberg, *Schizophrenic Germany* (New York, 1961), pp. 64–65.

16. Craig, *The Germans,* pp. 244–246.

17. Ronald F. Bunn, *German Politics and the Spiegel Affair* (Louisiana, 1968). p. 31.

18. Klaus Bölling, *Republic in Suspense* (New York, 1964), pp. 180–183.

19. Richard Hiscocks, *The Adenauer Era* (Philadelphia, 1966), p. 249.

20. David Schoenbaum, *The Spiegel Affair* (New York, 1968), p. 100.

21. Hiscocks, p. 251.

22. Strauss' obituary is recorded in the *New York Times,* October 4, 1988. See also the *Chronik der Stadt München,* 28 August 1979.

23. The delegates came from Bavaria, Bremen, Hessen, and Württemberg-Baden, the states that made up the American Zone of Occupation. See John Gimbel, "The Origins of the *Institut für Zeitgeschichte:* Scholarship, Politics, and the

American Occupation, 1945–1949." *American Historical Review,* 1965, vol. LXX, pp. 714–731.

24. On popular culture in Munich after the war, see the *New York Times* article, "Munich Restored Bigger than Ever." April 26, 1959, p. 26.

25. Brandt, pp. 84–85. Each locker holds one stein and every member that has a locker has his or her own key. Once a year, every member must appear at the *Hofbräuhaus* office and pay the rent for the locker in person, or else they can loose the locker. In 1997 the annual rent was 6 Marks. See also *Hofbräuhaus 1897–1997,* p. 52 for the number of mugs stolen in the 1960s.

26. Bauer, et al.; *Geschichte der Stadt München,* p. 417.

27. This of course was in addition to reparations, rebuilding destroyed synagogues, and returning as much as possible confiscated Jewish property. See *München Arisiert,* p. 233.

28. See the August 1972 edition, vol. 19, no. 8; pp. 132–144; 180–183 It offers an article with some history and lots of advice on how and where to meet the local women. The *Hofbräuhaus* is not mentioned.

29. Thanks to the income from the Olympics, it took less than ten years to transform the infrastructure of Munich. Without this income, city planners estimated that it would have taken over twenty years to complete a project of such magnitude. See *US News and World Report,* "International Report" August 21, 1972, pp. 58–59.

30. In English, the most recent book on the 1972 Munich Olympic tragedy is Simon Reeve, *One Day in September* (New York, 2000). He points out that the Germans were at pains to ensure that the 1972 Olympics would erase the memory of the 1936 (Nazi) Berlin Olympics, but seems to suggest that the Germans could have avoided the whole disaster with better security and a better rescue attempt. In German, see Bauer, *Geschichte der Stadt München,* pp. 417–418. Both authors agree that the terrorist attack at Munich was a terrible disappointment for the city and the Olympic planners because it resurrected all the ghosts of the past that Germany sought to overcome, above all the massacre of Jews on German soil.

31. Brandt, p. 106–107.

32. See Turner, pp. 170–171. That this kind of domestic terrorism was a European problem, see Walter Laqueur, *Europe in Our Time* (New York, 1992), p. 446–448.

33. See Large, pp. 360–361. For the broader European context, see Laqueur, p. 459. In the spring 2005 Bavarian police broke up a Neo-Nazi ring, the "Kamaradschaft Süd" that planned to bomb the Jewish Center of Munich. *Sueddeutsche.de,* March 2, 2005 and April 4, 2004.

34. See the *Hofbräuhaus 400. Jahre Festschrift,* p. 127.

35. *Hofbräuhaus, 400 Jahre Festschrift,* pp. 174–195.

36. See the *Hofbräuhaus* www site (www.hofbraeuhaus.de) history, "1988." The new facility would be capable of double the production of the former brewery facility.

9. *400 Years of* Gemütlichkeit

1. The commemorative video and CD "*In München steht ein Hofbräuhaus*" was issued by Pantoffel-Kino (video) and München-Ariola (CD) and ZDF. See also *Hofbräuhaus Munchen: 1589–1989: 400 Jahre Tradition Festschrift* (Carl Gerber Verlag, München, 1989).

2. This debunks the myth that only tourists visit the Hofbräuhaus. Taken from an interview with Michael Sperger "Ein Spaziergang durchs Hofbräuhaus" an information guide to Munich's most famous beer hall published 1980. See also the HB 1897–1997, p. 53.

3. The testimonials are recorded in the *Hofbräuhaus 400. Jahre Festschrift*, pp. 5–7.

4. Walter Laquer rightly notes that the East German revolts of 1989 marked a genuine revolution from the street. See Laquer, *Europe in Our Time* (New York 1992), p. 555.

5. For his efforts, Masur was later asked to stand for President of East Germany, but he refused. See "There's more to Maestro Masur than Music" in *The Wall Street Journal/Europe,* April 20–21, 1990, p. 7.

6. It was impossible to close them again by morning. See Henry A. Turner, *Germany from Partition to Reunification* (New Haven, 1992), p. 234.

7. At one border crossing alone, Rudolfstein-Hirsching, 180,000 East Germans crossed into the west that weekend. The East Germans were given DM 100. "Greeting Money" which was usually matched by the Bavarian government so that Easterners had some money to spend. At least 7000 easterners made their way to Munich that first weekend of freedom. See "Der Luft is voller Jubel" in the *Süddeutsche Zeitung,* 13 November 1989, p. 5.

8. "AmWochenende 6000 DDR-Burger Feierten im Hofbräuhaus" in the *Bild Zeitung,* 13 November 1989, p. 7.

9. These figures are recorded in the *Münchener StadtChronik* of December 1989 held at the *Stadtarchiv* Munich.

10. Hofbraeuhaus.de "1995"

11. "Gorbi, Gorbi" München lag dem ex-Präsidenten zu Füßen" *Tageszeitung,* 23 January 2001 (Online at www.hofbraeuhaus.de).

12. "Jubiläumsspeisekarte der Münchener Innenstadtwirte" 15–30 June 1997. The special menu also featured the specials of all the other restaurants participating in the event, some fifteen restaurants in all.

13. Above all, the best source for the Hofbräuhaus' transformation between 1897–1997 is Bernd Kirschner (ed.), *100 Jahre Hofbräuhaus am Platzl in München in Seiner heutigen Weltberühmten Gestalt.* (Starnberg, 1997). Other information on the festivities have been obtained from the www.hofbraeuhaus.de site See also, "Hofbräuhaus: Ein Mythos wird 100 in the Süddeutschezeitung, 4 November 1997, p. 35. The plans for the anniversary celebrations were explained to the members in a letter from Michael Sperger, of November 1997. The event even made the papers in the United States. See the *New York Daily News,* August 10, 1997 "Happy Birthday at Munich Hofbräuhaus."

14. "W. German Beer Law Brouhaha" *Newsday,* 12 July 1984, p. 45.

15. See hofbraeuhaus.de (History, "1999"). Also, see "Local Beer in Munich will Soon be Belgian" in *The New York Times,* 20 September 2003, pp. c1–c3.

16. See Fenzl, p. 282.

17. For the "Beer Garden Revolution" see Eckelt, *Biergeschichte(n)*, pp. 126–127; see also "Noch ein Bier und noch eins- bis Mitternacht" in *Sueddeutsche.de*, 10 May 2005. The decision to allow beer gardens to stay open until midnight was announced in June 2005. See the *Sueddeutsche Zeitung Online*, "Bis Mitternacht im Biergarten- Ein Testlauf" 21 June 2005.

18. See Fenzl, pp. 263–266. The slogan of the demonstration was "No! A City Says No!" See also Large, *Where Ghosts Walked*, pp. 347–362.

19. The *Hofbräuhaus* Cincinnati actually ended up in Newport Kentucky, less than ten minutes from downtown Cincinnati (www.hofbrauhausnewport.com), The *Hofbräuhaus* Las Vegas, which opened in April 2004, is directly across from the Hard Rock Café and Casino. (www.LasVegas.com). See also the *HB Zapfhahn*, vol 1, May 2003, pp. 7–10; and vol. 2, September 2003, pp. 4 & 12. The Gastager brothers from Munich own and operate the *Hofbräuhaus* Las Vegas. For their interview, see *The Atlantic Times*, "A Hofbräuhaus in Vegas" May 2005, p. 15.

20. "Schweigen für Amerika" in the *Süddeutsche Zeitung* 14 September 2001 (from Sueddeutsche.de).

21. "Jetzt kommen die Amis wieder" in the *Süddeutsche Zeitung*, 26 August 2004 (from Sueddeutsche.de).

22. See Fenzl, p. 278. At least in the inner city, the old town, skyscrapers continue to be forbidden, but the jury is still out regarding outer parts of the city. See also "27.000 Unterschriften gegen die neuen Hochhäuser" in *Sueddeutsche.de*, 8 July 2004. The Siemens company planned to build a large corporate development called "Isar South" with skyscrapers, to which several thousand Münchener's said "no."

23. See "Die neuen alten Wirte vom Hofbräuhaus" 14 July 2004 (online: www.sueddeutsche.de).

24. "Sklaverei im Hofbräu," *Sueddeutsche.de*, 13 May 2004.

25. "US Tourist wegen Masskrug-Diebstahl vier Wochen in Haft" in *Spiegel Online*, 20 August 2004. The court also admonished the prosecutor for even bringing the case, claiming that trying to steal a mug from the *Hofbräuhaus* has become like a "sport."

26. At least as long as it keeps making money, the State of Bavaria has no intention of selling the world's most famous beer hall. The *Hofbräuhaus* remains Bavaria's "sacred [cash] cow." See "Ministerschutz fur die Heilige Kuh" in *Sueddeutsche.de*, 23 February 2005.

27. Cited in the *Hofbräuhaus Zapfhahn*, # 4, 2005.

28. The new sports complex cost 340 million euro; Herzog & De Meuron, architects. The arena has become a tourist attraction on the north side of town as people from all over the world come to admire the futuristic architecture. See "Die Heimschwache nach dem Spiel" in *Sueddeutsche Zeitung*, December 29, 2005 (Sueddeutsche.de).

29. "Neun Millionen Touristen, null Hooligans" in *Sueddeutsche Zeitung*, July 6, 2006 (Sueddeutsche.de). See also, "Nichts regt sich im Bordell" *Sueddeutsche Zeitung*, July 3, 2006 (sueddeutsche.de); and "World Cup brings Little Pleasure to German Brothels" by Mark Landler. The *New York Times*, July 3, 2006; On

the production of the *Hofbräuhaus* and its relation to the World Cup, see www.hofbraeuhaus.de.

30. "A Unifier Not a Divider: Germany's Ballack Bridges East and West." By Jere Longman, *New York Times,* June 29, 2006. pp. D1-D2. The author suggests that the composition of the team, and the increasing visibility of Eastern Germans in politics and culture suggests "how far the country has come . . . and how far it has to go" before the psychological divisions of post-wall Germany disappear. See also "Divided Without a Wall: Germans are Now Split By a Rift of the Mind" by Peter Beaumont. *The Observer,* April 3, 2005. (www.observer.co.uk). The author notes that 1/4 of West Germans and half that number of East Germans wanted to put the Wall back up as late as 2005. The World Cup Games may have changed these numbers. See "Es War nur Fußball" in the *Sueddeutsche Zeitung,* July 8, 2006 (Sueddeutsche.de).

31. Even Gunter Grass, a less than enthusiastic supporter of German reunification in the 1990s, marveled at the "unclenched cheerfulness" of the mood in Germany during the games. See "Germany Emerges as World Champion of Good Cheer" by Roger Cohen. *New York Times,* July 9, 2006 (Sports), p. 8.

Bibliography

Primary Sources, Catalogs, and Archival Material

1589–1989 400 Jahre Hofbräuhaus München. Anniversary Festschrift for the 400 anniversary of Munich's Hofbräuhaus, Munich, 1989.

375 Jahre Münchner Hofbräuhaus Festschrift, Munich, 1964.

1589–1939 350 Jahre Hofbräuhaus München. Anniversary festschrift for the 350th anniversary of Munich's Hofbräuhaus, Munich, 1939.

"Ein Berliner Ein Stündchen im Münchener Hofbräuhaus: True Stories." In München, vol 23. Munich, 1923(?). (Princeton University Library).

Ferdl, Weiß. "Die Linie 8" CD production of Ferdl's famous acts produced by BMG/Ariola Media, Munich, 1991.

Das Münchener Hofbräuhaus Einst und Jetzt. Munich, 1923(?) (Princeton University Library).

"In München steht ein Hofbräuhaus" Video and CD publication to commemorate 400th anniversary of Hofbräuhaus. Munich, 1989: München-Ariola Media and ZDF.

"München: Hauptstadt der Bewegung" (ed.). Catalogue to exhibition Münchener Stadtmuseum. Dr. Wolfgang Till, editor, Munich 1993.

Lengl, Siegfried (ed.). *Der Freistaat Bayern.* Catalog to exhibit with historical essays. Munich, Hanns-Seidel Foundation and the Bavarian Ministry of Culture, 1970.

Platzl Bühne: Festschrift 85. Jahre. Munich, 1991.

Roesseler, August. *Das Hofbräuhaus München.* Munich 1927. (Library of Congress).

Stadtchronik der Stadt München. Online: Muenchen.de/Rathaus/dir/stadtarchiv/chronik.

Stadtchronik der Stadt München: 1989, volumes 1–4, Stadtarchiv München.

Staatsarchiv München. "Hofbräuhaus München" Files 1–11 in series.

Wirtshäuser in München um 1900 (edited catalog with various essays on the beer halls and restaurants of Munich), Buchendorfer Press, 1997.

Secondary Literature

Baer, Fritz. *Die Minister-Präsidenten Bayerns*. Munich, 1971.

Bailey, George. *Munich*. Amsterdam, 1980.

Barrows, Susanna and Robin Room. *Drinking: Behavior and Belief in Modern History* (Los Angeles, 1991).

Bauer, Reinhard and Ernst Piper (ed.). *München: Ein Lesebuch*. Frankfurt/Main, 1986.

Bauer, Richard (ed.). *Geschichte der Stadt München*. Munich, 1992.

Bauer, Richard. *Geschichte Münchens*. Munich 2003.

Baumann, Angelika (ed.). *München Arisiert*. Munich, 2004.

Baumann-Oelwein, Cornelia. *Der Orlandoblock am Münchener Platzl* Munich, 2000.

Bolling, Klaus. *Republic in Suspense*. New York, 1964.

Botting, Douglas. *From the Ruins of the Reich*. New York, 1985.

Brandt, Paul, *Das Münchener Hofbräuhaus*. Dachau, 1997.

Brantl, Klaus. *Strahlendes München*. Munich, 1960.

Broszat, Martin (ed.). *Bayern in der NS-Zeit*. Munich, 1981.

Bunn, Ronald F. *German Politics and the Spiegel Affair*. Louisiana, 1968.

Cassidy, David. *Uncertainty: A Life of Werner Heisenberg*. New York, 1991.

Cassidy, David. *Einstein and Our World*, New York, 2004.

Channon, Henry. *The Ludwigs of Bavaria*. London, 1952.

Chapman-Houston, Desmond. *Ludwig II: The Mad King of Bavaria*. New York, 1993.

Craig, Gordon A. *Germany 1866–1945*. Oxford, 1978.

Craig, Gordon A. *The Germans*. New York, 1983.

Deming, Brian and Ted Iliff, *Hitler and Munich*. Berchesgaden, 1980.

Dix, Rudi. *München: Das waren die fünfziger*. Munich, 1994.

Dornberg, John. *Schizophrenic Germany*. New York, 1961.

Dornberg, John. *Munich 1923*. New York, 1982.

Dornbusch, Horst. *Prost! The Story of German Beer*. Boulder, 1997.

Dunn, Richard S. *The Age of Religious Wars, 1559–1715*. New York. 1979.

Eckelt, Birgit, *Biergeschichte(n): bayerns fünftes Element*. Rosenheim, 1999.

Farago, Ladislas. *Patton: Ordeal and Triumph*. New York, 1963.

Fenzl, Fritz, *Münchener Stadtgeschichten*. Munich, 2004.

Friedrich, Carl J. *The Age of Baroque, 1610–1660*. New York, 1952.

Fruhstorfer, Georg and Heidi. *Hurra, Wir Leben Noch! München nach 1945*. Munich 2003.

Fürstenau, Justus. *Entnazifierung*. Berlin, 1969.

Gaab, Jeffrey S. *Justice Delayed The Restoration of Justice in Bavaria under American Occupation, 1945–1949*. New York, 1999.

Gieshofer, Franz (ed.). *Die Lederhose*. Munich, 1996.

Gritschneder, Otto. *Pater Rupert Mayer vor dem Sondergericht*. Munich, 1974.

Gritschneder, Otto. *Kardinal Michael von Faulhaber zwischen Widerstand und Anpassung*. Munich, 1979.

Grunberger, Richard. *The Twelve Year Reich,* New York, 1971.

Grunberger, Richard. *Red Rising in Bavaria*. London, 1973.

Gutman, Robert. *Richard Wagner: The Man, His Mind, His Music*. New York, 1990.

Gutman, Robert. *Mozart. A Cultural Biography*. New York, 1991.

Hamilton, Nigel. *John F. Kennedy: Reckless Youth*. New York, 1992.

Haverkamp, Alfred. *Medieval Germany: 1056–1273*. Oxford, 1992.

Hawthorne, Larry. *The Beer Drinker's Guide to Munich.* Honolulu, 2000.

Hayman, Ronald. *Hitler and Geli.* New York, 1997.

Hitler, Adolf. *Mein Kampf.* New York, 1971.

Hitzer, Friedrich, *Der Mord im Hofbräuhaus.* Frankfurt/Main, 1981.

Hiscocks, Richard. *The Adenauer Era.* Philadelphia, 1966.

Hoffmann, Peter. *The History of the German Resistance, 1933–1945.* Cambridge, 1977.

Holborn, Hajo. *A History of Modern Germany.* Princeton, 1969.

Horstmann, G. Henry. *Consular Reminiscences.* Philadelphia, 1886.

Huber, Brigitte (ed.). *Tagebuch der Stadt München 1818–2000.* Munich 2004.

Joachimsthaler, Anton. *Hitler's Weg begann in München 1913–1923.* Munich, 2000.

Kershaw, Ian. *Hitler: 1889–1936, "Hubris."* New York, 1999.

Kershaw, Ian. *Hitler: 1936–1945, "Nemesis."* New York, 2000.

Kirchner, Bernd (ed.). *1897–1997 100 Jahre Hofbräuhaus am Platzl in München* Pocking/Starnberg, 1997.

Lacquer, Walter. *Europe in Our Time.* New York, 1992.

Large, David Clay. *Where Ghosts Walked: Munich's Road to the Third Reich* New York, 1997.

Large, David Clay. *The Politics of Law and Order: A History of the Bavarian Einwohnerwehr, 1918–1921.* Philadelphia, 1980.

Malenowski, Wolfgang (ed.). *1945: Deutschland im Stunde Null.* Hamburg, 1985.

Mitchell, Allen. *Revolution in Bavaria: 1918–1919.* Princeton, 1965.

Oelwein, Cornelia, *Das Münchener Platzl.* Munich, 2003.

Ozment, Steven. *Protestants: The Birth of a Revolution.* New York, 1991.

Pope, Ernest R. *Munich Playground.* New York, 1953.

Prinz, Friedrich. *Die Geschichte Bayerns.* Munich, 1997.

Prinz, Friedrich (ed.). *Trümmerzeit in München.* Munich, 1984.

Reeve, Simon. *One Day in September.* New York, 2000.

Reichlmayr, Georg and Rudolf Ites, *München: Eine kurzer Stadtgeschichte.* Erfurt, 2001.

Rice, Eugene F. *The Foundations of Early Modern Europe.* New York, 1970.

Ripley, LaVerne. *The German-Americans.* Boston, 1976.

Rosenfeld, Gavriel. *Munich and Memory.* Berkeley, 2000.

Ruhm von Oppen, Beate (Ed). *Documents on Germany under Occupation, 1945–1954.* New York, 1955.

Sackett, Robert E. *Popular Entertainment, Class, and Politics in Munich 1900–1923.* Cambridge, 1982.

Sadie, Stanley. *Mozart.* New York, 1982.

Schattenhofer, Michael. *München: 1870–1910.* Frankfurt/Main 1980.

Schoenbaum, David. *The Spiegel Affair.* New York, 1968.

Seymour, Bruce. *Lola Montez: A Life.* New Haven, 1996.

Sheehan, James J. *German History 1770–1866.* Oxford, 1989.

Spahn, Boris. *München: Hauptstadt der Bewegung.* Munich, 1939.

Stock, Birgit and Rainer. *Der Biercomik: Die Geschichte vom Hofbräuhaus in München.* Munich 2004.

Taylor, Telford. *Munich: The Price of Peace.* New York, 1979.

Thoma, Ludwig. *An Angel from Munich.* Munich 1988.

Trautmann, Franz. *Legends and Tales of Old Munich.* Munich, 1958.

Tuchel, Johannes. *Lexicon des Wiederstandes 1933–1945.* Munich, 1994.

Turner, Henry A. *Germany from Partition to Reunification.* New Haven, 1992.

Tworek, Elizabeth. *Bayerisches Lesebuch*. Munich, 1999.

Walker, Mack. *Germany and the Emigration*. Cambridge, 1964.

Waite, Robert G. L. *Vanguard of Nazism: The Freikorps Movement in Postwar Germany, 1918–1923*. New York, 1952.

Waite, Robert G. L. *Psychopathic God Adolf Hitler*. New York, 1977.

Wistrich, Robert. *Weekend in Munich*. London, 1995.

Wolf, Thomas. *The Web and the Rock*. New York, 1937.

Ziegler, Philip. *The Black Death*. New York, 1969.

Index